Ur

Archaeological Histories

Series editor: Thomas Harrison

An important series charting the history of sites, buildings and towns from their construction to the present day. Each title examines not only the physical history and uses of the site but also its broader context: its role in political history, in the history of scholarship, and in the popular imagination.

Tarquinia, Robert Leighton
Avebury, Joshua Pollard & Mark Gillings
Pompeii, Alison E. Cooley

Ur

The City of the Moon God

Harriet Crawford

Bloomsbury Academic
An imprint of Bloomsbury Publishing Plc

B L O O M S B U R Y
LONDON • NEW DELHI • NEW YORK • SYDNEY

Bloomsbury Academic

An imprint of Bloomsbury Publishing Plc

50 Bedford Square	1385 Broadway
London	New York
WC1B 3DP	NY 10018
UK	USA

www.bloomsbury.com

BLOOMSBURY and the Diana logo are trademarks of Bloomsbury Publishing Plc

First published 2015

British Library Cataloguing-in-Publication Data
A catalogue record for this book is available from the British Library.

ISBN: HB: 978-1-47253-369-2
PB: 978-1-47252-419-5
ePDF: 978-1-47252-219-1
ePub: 978-1-47253-169-8

Library of Congress Cataloging-in-Publication Data
A catalog record for this book is available from the Library of Congress.

Typeset by Fakenham Prepress Solutions, Fakenham, Norfolk NR21 8NN
Printed and bound in Great Britain

Contents

List of Illustrations

Acknowledgements

My warmest thanks go to Fran Reynolds who set the ball rolling and to Tom Harrison who picked it up! I am also very grateful to Tessa Rickards and Mary Shepperson who drew the figures and to Charlotte Loveridge and Anna MacDiarmid at Bloomsbury who have been unfailingly helpful and supportive. My husband has allowed me to bore him rigid with queries, mainly about spelling and punctuation, and never lost his temper. Two external readers picked me up on a number of valuable points. Thank you all.

The Rediscovery of Ur

To many Europeans in the nineteenth and early twentieth centuries, the name Ur of the Chaldees conjured up an image of the archetypal mysterious Orient peopled by bearded figures in long white robes or wild tribesmen on fine horses. To Iraqis today, Ur is one of the oldest and most important of their heritage sites. Thanks to many years of meticulous work by scholars, we now know that the real settlement of Ur flourished for more than 5,000 years, and, for much of that time, was an important political and economic centre. This longevity was the result of its geographical position at the head of the Persian Gulf. This gave Ur control of one of the most important early trade routes that brought metals and many other goods into the Mesopotamian heartland. Control of the metals trade in particular undoubtedly gave Ur considerable political leverage, although other, less important, land-based trade routes existed as well. In addition, the trade brought great wealth to the city – wealth which is evident in the monuments and artefacts recovered from the site.

To the north-west the Euphrates connected Ur directly to the Anatolian heartland, making it one of the most strategically placed of the early cities. Few others could boast of such excellent internal and external connections. Ur's heyday came in the second half of the third millennium BC when its rulers competed on equal terms with the other cities of the plain and eventually imposed their rule over the whole area, creating what has been called the earliest empire in the region. After its destruction, in about 1800 BC, the city's trading links, coupled with the standing of its divine patron, the Moon God Sin, led to a swift rebuilding and a new life as a regional capital. It was only the retreat of the Gulf coast southwards and then the migration of the course of the river eastwards that caused Ur's abandonment.

The early fame of Ur in the West was due to the description in Genesis 11.8–31, which says that the city was the birthplace of Abraham, the founding father of

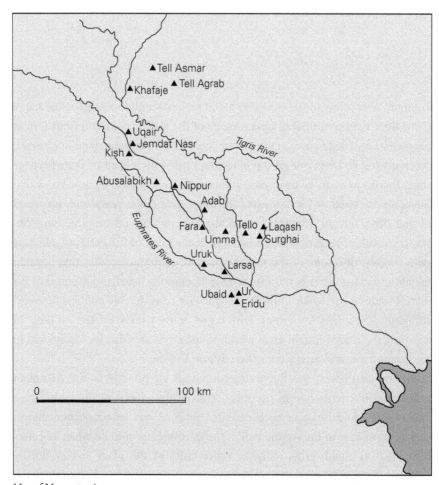

Map of Mesopotamia

the Jewish people. On this timescale its identification with a group of mounds ten miles west of the Euphrates in what is now a sandy desert in southern Iraq is relatively recent (Map 1). The first European to visit the site was probably Pietro della Valle, the early seventeenth-century Italian traveller who, when he eventually returned home, brought back with him bricks with cuneiform inscriptions, which no one could read, and a number of cylinder seals. In the early nineteenth century, under the Ottoman Empire, interest revived among Europeans in identifying the exact place where the ancient city had stood. A number of candidates were proposed, of which the favourite was a tell called variously Umghyer, Mughyer, Múgeyer, or Tell el-Mukayyar, the hill of pitch/bitumen. Bitumen was used instead of mortar in some of the exposed brickwork and this gave the tell its name. The site was visited in 1835 by J. Baillie Fraser, who described the two-storey construction at the heart of the mound, later to be identified as the ziggurat, or temple tower, and paced out its dimensions.

A certain amount of confusion was caused by various misidentifications, first by Sir Henry Rawlinson, the remarkable diplomat and scholar, who was one of the first to translate cuneiform. He initially proposed that Uruk/Warka was the biblical city of Ur. Later, Colonel Chesney, who was in charge of the ill-fated 'Expedition for the survey of the rivers Euphrates and Tigris', proposed a more elaborate idea. The expedition had set out in 1835 in two ironclad paddle steamers to navigate the length of the Euphrates from Birejik in modern Syria to the head of the Persian Gulf. The report of the expedition, which it was hoped would provide a shorter and more convenient passage to India, was not published for fifteen years because of various problems. When it did appear, Chesney claimed that the city of O'rfáh (Urfa) in Syria was the biblical Ur, perhaps because there is a strong local tradition that Abraham was born there; the cave in which this was said to have happened is still a sacred place today. He also suggested that the name then apparently migrated to Kal'ah Sherkát (close to modern Ashur), and finally came to rest in the area around Mujáyah, as he called it. 'The mound of Mujáyah, it is presumed, marks the site of the ancient capital of Aur, the Orchoe of Ptolemy ...' A further layer of uncertainty was added by the biblical tradition which also associated the name of Abraham with Harran (Gen. 11.31), near modern Urfa.

Even after the correct identification of the site by Rawlinson as a result of his decipherment of cuneiform inscriptions on bricks brought back by W. K. Loftus after a visit there in 1849, some doubts remained. In the inscription Rawlinson also recognized the name of the god Sin, the moon god to whom the ziggurat was dedicated, and the name of an area of the city called Ibra, which he took to be the same word as Abraham. A consensus was finally reached, largely as a result of Woolley's work, and the identification of Tell el-Mukayyar with Ur is now generally accepted.

The interest caused by this identification resulted in 1854 in the British Museum employing J. E. Taylor, the British vice-consul in Basra, to investigate various sites in southern Iraq, including Ur. Permission had to be obtained from the sultan in Constantinople for such work and many of the finds found their way to the imperial treasury there. Taylor's *Report to the Royal Asiatic Society* in 1854 described the ziggurat with its buttresses and air holes in the walls. He identified two storeys and found many fragments of blue-glazed bricks and copper nails on the top of the mound, but his most important finds were four well-preserved foundation cylinders of Nabonidus of Babylon. These were buried by the king at the four corners of the ziggurat when he restored it, and he was also responsible for the blue-glazed bricks, which had probably faced the top storey. In addition, Taylor dug what he thought was a house with a narrow, arched door, but which later work showed was part of the Gate of Judgement, or *E-dub-lal-mah*, where justice was dispensed at one of the entrances to the inner court of Nanna. He also recognized many other mounds lying south of the ziggurat as part of the city. Sadly, after Taylor's second season when he worked mainly at Eridu, where another ziggurat was found, the British Museum decided to concentrate their efforts and their money in Assyria, where the pickings for museums were much richer. It was as a result of this work in the north that the museum acquired its magnificent collection of Assyrian palace reliefs. Work in the south did not begin again for more than sixty years.

Looking back, we can see that these pioneering explorers achieved a good deal. They showed beyond doubt that the early civilizations of Mesopotamia had built large cities with monumental buildings in the inhospitable south as well as in the more fertile northern plains of Iraq. These men worked with no training and little equipment, in a hostile environment where water was short and sandstorms a common occurrence. It was also dangerous, as their camps could be prowled around by lions or by desert raiders, and the workforce was usually made up of local people whose attitude varied between mild curiosity and outright hostility. It was also dangerous for the tells they explored, as there was also a pervasive feeling that these strange foreigners must be looking for gold. This belief was bound to lead to theft, illicit digging and the plundering of sites.

The site of Ur itself is not welcoming. It lies 220 miles south of Baghdad and about 10 miles west of the modern course of the Euphrates in a low-lying wasteland of dunes and sand. It used to be close to the Basra to Baghdad railway, part of the proposed Berlin to Basra line that was never completed. It was possible to get off the train from Baghdad at the grandly named Ur Junction, where a branch line turned off to Nasariyah, and drive a mere two miles across the desert to the site itself, but the station was closed sometime after the Second World War, leaving a long, hot journey in a four-wheeled vehicle as the only option. It is now apparent, with the advantages provided by satellite photographs and modern boring equipment, that its surroundings were very different in the past. At the time the settlement was founded, in the Ubaid period from the late sixth to late fifth millenna BC, the level of the Persian Gulf was rising, and by the Uruk period a 1,000 years or so later, the water was 2.5 metres above today's level with the coastline reaching as far as Ur itself, creating new marshes and a new delta. Pournelle, an expert in the interpretation of satellite photographs, describes these early settlements like Ur as 'islands embedded in a marshy plain, situated on the borders and in the heart of vast deltaic marshlands … Their waterways served less as irrigation canals than as transport routes'. Loftus, writing in 1857, states that even then, 'During inundation [Ur] was completely surrounded by water', and Mallowan in the 1920s observed the same phenomenon.

This conjures up a rather different picture from the one we see today and suggests that the economy of the early settlement here, and in other comparable locations in southern Iraq, was largely dependent on the surrounding marshes for survival. The marshes provided food, fish, birds, edible tubers and much else, as well as raw materials such as reeds, which were used for everything from roofing to boats, containers, fodder and fuel. Crops could also be sown on the tops of the levees, or turtle backs as they are called by Pournelle, and date trees cultivated, but these were initially of less economic significance. The marshes may not have been the healthiest locations, but they were extraordinarily rich in the essentials of early village – and even urban – life.

With the recent recognition of the vital importance of the marshes as a sustaining environment for these early settlers, it has to be asked if the introduction of agriculture had the transforming effect on society that is generally assumed. It could be argued that agriculture becomes less significant as a stimulant for the development of the first villages in the deltaic region and overturns many of our previous assumptions about the so-called agricultural revolution. The proposed picture of the vital importance of the marshes is supported by the earliest texts from the end of the fourth millennium. Although agriculture was well established by then, the texts still stress the importance of fish and reeds to the local economies. The settlements began to trade as a means of acquiring materials the marshes could not supply.

By the early second millennium, the waters of the Gulf began to retreat after a series of fluctuations, and the subsistence balance shifted irrevocably towards irrigation, agriculture and animal husbandry as the most important sources of essential foods. Trade continued to grow and, as we shall see, the site of Ur boasted two harbours, one on the river and one on a canal, to facilitate travel and trade. As the head of the Gulf retreated southwards, access to the important maritime route down the Persian Gulf must have become more difficult. This factor almost certainly contributed to the economic decay of the city.

Fifty years and more after Taylor left Ur, archaeological work was restarted in 1918 after the First World War, when the presence of British troops brought some security to the region. The situation was very different in other ways too. Archaeology was becoming a profession in its own right for which training and certain skills were becoming essential, rather than being seen as an addendum to exploration. R. Campbell Thompson, who was serving as an Intelligence officer on the staff of the British Army in Mesopotamia, and who had previously been an assistant at the British Museum, went to Ur to undertake some experimental work for the museum. The results were sufficiently interesting for Dr Hall, also a wartime Intelligence officer, to be deputed to go to Ur the following year to carry out further excavations. Hall had started work at the British Museum in 1896 as an assistant to E. A. Wallis Budge, becoming Assistant Keeper, Department of Egyptian and Assyrian Antiquities, in 1919. He had extensive experience of digging in Egypt, as well as a good knowledge of the objects in the museum's collections, making him well equipped to dig at Ur.

Hall was given seventy Turkish prisoners of war, together with their Indian guards, to work for him. This detachment of soldiers was in addition to the local workers supplied by their sheikh. Hall needed to find ways to control a large and unskilled workforce with only the help of three NCOs (non-commissioned officers), none of whom had any archaeological experience. He achieved a remarkable amount in a season lasting about three months, especially when it is remembered that he also worked – though for much shorter periods – at Eridu and al Ubaid, where he uncovered some of the superb decorations fallen from the façade of a mid-third-millennium temple. At Ur, he uncovered the building, later to be identified as a possible palace, the *E-Hur-sag*, built within the sacred precinct that surrounded the ziggurat. He also traced the south-east face of the ziggurat itself. In addition, he retrieved numerous tablets and other small finds, and dug a number of graves, including some dating back to the late third millennium.

Hall's work was limited to a single season because the British Museum had no money to pay for further work – a frustrating situation familiar to many archaeologists since. In 1922, however, George Byron Gordon, the Director of the University Museum in Philadelphia, who knew of Hall's work, proposed that a joint expedition with the British Museum should be set up to work at Ur, and that Leonard Woolley, whom he knew already (see page 8), should be appointed to lead the expedition (Fig. 1.i). Woolley was to work at Ur for the next twelve years.

Charles Leonard Woolley was a clergyman's son, born in 1880. He went up as a scholarship boy to New College Oxford, intending to go into the church himself. However, he did less well academically than expected, and reluctantly gave up the idea of the ministry. He had no clear idea of what he would do instead, although he toyed with the idea of teaching. He describes how he became an archaeologist in the following paragraph:

> I have seldom been more surprised in my life than I was when the Warden of New College told me that he had decided I should be an archaeologist ... I must confess that when the prospect did present itself, not as a mere idea to be played with (for one did not lightly play with the Warden's decisions), but as something definite and settled, I was not altogether happy about it. I preferred the open air and was more interested in my fellow men than in dead-and-gone things.

As it turned out, the Warden had made an inspired decision.

Woolley began his archaeological career in 1905 as an assistant keeper in the Ashmolean Museum and had his first taste of fieldwork on Hadrian's Wall. In his second season in the area, he found the so-called Lion of Corbridge, proving that he already had that most important of archaeological assets: luck. However, three years later he left the Ashmolean and went to work for the University of Pennsylvania in the Nubian Desert. Here he was introduced to the Near East, to Arabic, and to the meticulous methods of excavation and recording used by Randall MacIver, who had been taught by Flinders Petrie himself. Later, Woolley was to use a version of Petrie's famous sequence-dating when excavating at Ur. The method had evolved when Petrie was digging a huge cemetery whose date was unknown. Petrie recorded the relative depth of each grave and of the pots found in them, arguing that those at the bottom of the sequence had to be the oldest. In this way he was able to build up a picture of which pots belonged where in the sequence and to use that relative dating to tie his cemetery to other better-dated sites where possible. This work in Nubia was also the beginning of an important partnership between Woolley and Pennsylvania that was cemented by a visit there in 1910.

1.i Portrait of Sir Leonard Woolley © National Portrait Gallery, London

Woolley's career progressed rapidly and, in 1912, he was appointed to lead a field expedition to Carchemish, under the aegis of the British Museum. He was accompanied by T. E. Lawrence as his assistant and they became great friends. Even more importantly, he had as his foreman a Syrian sheikh called Hamoudi, who was to work with him at Ur for many years. They formed a crucial partnership, and Woolley came to regard Hamoudi – and later his sons, too – with enormous affection and respect.

Because of its status as an important border crossing, Carchemish had been frequently destroyed during its history. The problems posed for an excavator by these destructions were compounded by some very bad digging by previous investigators. In spite of this, Woolley and Lawrence seem to have had an exciting time of it and indulged in a series of adventures which were pure Indiana Jones: putting a gun to the head of the local governor to get a permit, for example, and spying on the Germans for Naval Intelligence. The Germans were attempting to build the Berlin to Baghdad railway, which was to pass very close to Carchemish, in preparation for their planned domination of the Ottoman Empire after the First World War.

Surprisingly perhaps, given the circumstances, Woolley and Lawrence also made some significant archaeological finds, uncovering some fine wall reliefs in the palace of the neo-Hittite rulers, and tracing the fortification walls and a city gate. Woolley was simultaneously finishing work in Nubia, commuting between the two areas, and, in addition, using every opportunity to buy antiquities for the British Museum and smuggle them back to Britain.

Just before the war broke out in 1914, the pair was asked to undertake a survey of the Sinai desert. The survey was officially described as 'travelling in the footsteps of Moses', but was generally assumed to have been a rather thin cover for Intelligence work. Woolley already understood the importance of publication and even this jaunt was published, entitled *The Wilderness of Zin*. On their way home, the two young men managed to travel along a stretch of the new German railway through Turkey, before being ejected by the angry Germans.

With these experiences behind him, it was to be expected that when Woolley was commissioned in the Royal Field Artillery at the outbreak of war he found himself seconded to Military Intelligence. He was posted to Cairo, where he worked with Lawrence, and met Gertrude Bell, who was also working there, and who was to be important to him when he was digging at Ur. He was then posted to Alexandria, where he was put in charge of French and English spy ships in the eastern Mediterranean. One of these ships was captured by the Turks while Woolley was on board and he spent the next two years in a Turkish prisoner-of-war camp. The experience does not appear to have been too onerous, because his letters speak of plays, concerts and a camp newspaper. His work in Alexandria must have been useful to the war effort as he was subsequently awarded the French Croix de Guerre.

After the war Woolley returned to Carchemish and then, because of the political situation, went back to Egypt to work in the Amarna village. A string of articles appeared on both topics, some in the *Illustrated London News* and some in more scholarly publications. Woolley showed himself to be an excellent communicator and realized early in his career how important it was to engage the wider public, outside a narrow academic circle. This was especially true when trying to raise money for his projects, as he had to do at Ur.

Woolley's work at Carchemish – and especially what might be called his apprenticeship in Egypt, where standards of excavation were higher – played an extremely important part in training him for the gigantic task which lay ahead: leadership of the joint British Museum/Pennsylvania expedition to Ur in 1922 (Fig. 1.ii). The first season began that autumn. By modern standards the team was very small: Woolley himself; Hamoudi, who had worked as his foreman at Carchemish, and who, with his sons, was in charge of the workmen; a series of general assistants, of whom the best-known and longest-serving was Max Mallowan, later to become Professor, Sir Max; and a succession of epigraphists. There was usually an architectural draughtsman as well, to help with recording the buildings. This small team of Europeans was supported by anything up to 250 local workmen, who became extremely skilled over the years and were the backbone of the expedition. The men worked in gangs consisting of a pick-man and up to six basket men who carried the spoil away to the dumps. They worked from sunrise to sunset with time off for breakfast and lunch, but it was a tough job. Woolley drove his European team hard, too, and worked exceptionally hard himself. He also took considerable pains to train up his young assistants. Mallowan, in his memoirs, tells a story of how one evening he and another member of the team were playing cards. Woolley came up to them and told them that they should be either working or in to bed.

In 1924, the team was augmented by Mrs Katharine Keeling, a widow, who took over the housekeeping side of the expedition and proved to be a good draughtswoman who drew many of the finds. She was to become a pivotal figure in Woolley's life and seems to have been an extraordinary woman, with immense charisma. She was capable of charming money out of people's pockets to support Woolley's work. On the other hand, she is also said to have been a hypochondriac with a difficult and complex personality. A fictional character thought to have been based on Mrs Keeling appears in Agatha Christie's *Murder in Mesopotamia*. In the book, she is heartily disliked by the other characters and becomes the first murder victim. In 1927, Keeling and Woolley married, and from that time on, until her death in 1945, she seems to have ruled his life with a rod of iron, giving full rein to her hypochondria and her snobbishness.

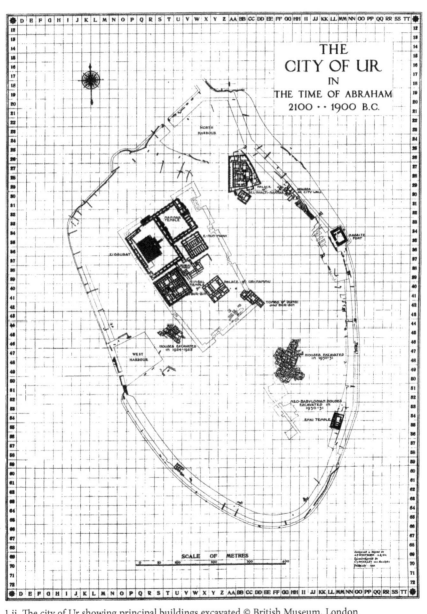

1.ii The city of Ur showing principal buildings excavated © British Museum, London

Woolley proved to be a remarkable excavator; his recording was meticulous in spite of the large number of untrained workmen and the small size of his team. Anyone who has worked on the remains from Ur will know how carefully he recorded what was found and how perceptive his comments could be, though there are also serious gaps in the information. He showed extraordinary imagination, as when he recovered the remains of the lyres from Grave PG1151. He poured plaster of Paris down a series of small holes that had appeared in the soil, which proved to be all that was left of the frames of the wooden instruments. The plaster of Paris, when hard, retained the instruments' original shapes, together with the inlays which had decorated them. He also showed great self-control when, in the first season, the workmen stumbled on part of the royal cemetery. Woolley felt that they were not expert enough to tackle the complex tasks presented by the graves and took them off the area until four seasons later, by which time he judged them to have gained sufficient experience.

The finds from Ur were remarkably rich and varied. Under the law current at the time the excavations were being undertaken, half of all the finds remained in Iraq and the rest were divided between the British Museum and the Pennsylvania University Museum, the dig sponsors. The division at the end of each season was a rather fraught affair, with the redoubtable Gertrude Bell and Woolley himself haggling over which objects should go the new Iraq National Museum. Bell had set up the museum and was its first director. The law has since been changed and all objects must now stay in Iraq.

Woolley was outstandingly good at communicating his finds to the outside world, both by writing about them (often in the *Illustrated London News* and academic journals) and by lecturing, or when showing visitors round the site. He had a vivid imagination, but his judgement, and sometimes his interpretations, were coloured by his strong religious beliefs. When a thick, water-laid level was found in a deep pit (see Chapter 2) there was no doubt in his mind that it represented the actual remains of Noah's Flood. He would also firmly describe one of the houses dated to about 2000 BC as Abraham's house.

Woolley's remarkable achievements were recognized by the award of a knighthood in 1935. Those who knew him in his old age speak of his charm, his kindness, his impish sense of humour and his dedication to his work. He was correcting the proofs of his last article in 1960 shortly before he died. As we have seen, he was also entertaining and a brilliant communicator, but his personal life was not happy. In old age, after various misfortunes, including the death of his wife and being cited as co-respondent in a very messy divorce, things changed and he seems to have become a contented man. It is tempting to suggest that he was not a great judge of character and that, perhaps, in some ways he never really grew up, retaining a 'Peter Pan' charm to the end of his life. There can, however, be no doubt that he transformed our knowledge of the early art and history of southern Mesopotamia and left a legacy which will be difficult to surpass. The history of Ur as we know it today is witness to that.

The Earliest Levels at Ur

It is very difficult, if not impossible, to find traces of the first people to exploit the rich reserves of fish and game in southern Mesopotamia. No one has yet succeeded and realistically may never do so, because over the millennia the fertile silt from the rivers has covered the original surface of the plain many metres deep. In addition, the water level has risen, thus flooding the earliest deposits. To add another complication, the marshes in the extreme south of the country have expanded and contracted over time, adding more silt and making archaeological survey of the region almost impossible. We can only guess about the first people who came to exploit the rich hunting and fishing in and around the marshes, and left a minimal 'footfall' on the environment. They probably built shelters of reeds, had few personal possessions, and moved on regularly from one place to another in pursuit of food. Sadly, none of these characteristics would leave much of a mark in the archaeological record.

If such early foragers existed, there is another puzzle: we have no idea where they might have come from; if there was a single group of incomers, or a number of them. We have no evidence for the origins of these proposed early explorers. If several groups were involved, they may have drifted into the region from many directions – from north Mesopotamia, for example; from Syria; from Iran; or the shores of the Arabian Peninsula. All would have been attracted by the abundant wildlife. The earliest written records use a form of picture writing to convey simple information, usually economic in nature, but it is impossible to tell what language they are written in. By the time we have the earliest translatable written records in the early third millennium, the language spoken and written was Sumerian. This raises new questions. There has been much debate, over the years, about when the Sumerians arrived in Mesopotamia. There is considerable continuity in the material culture of the south from the late fifth to the end of the fourth millennium and this continuity might suggest that the Sumerians were present from the time of the earliest settlers. The early texts also retain elements of other languages, perhaps spoken by some of the other early groups to enter the region. It seems that this mixture of peoples and languages was responsible for the flowering of what is known as Sumerian culture in the third millennium BC: one of the most innovative and exciting cultures the world has ever known, and in which the city of Ur played an important role.

All we know for certain is that by the early sixth millennium, the fog that obscures the earliest history of south Mesopotamia begins to lift. The first people for whom there is evidence seem to have settled in small groups on some of the so-called 'turtlebacks', the slightly higher ridges of land rising above the waters of the marshes. So far there is no evidence that any of these early inhabitants experimented with agriculture, as their older contemporaries had done further north, since they seem to have already had the necessary skill to grow crops, and to have brought barley and einkorn wheat with them. This was probably necessary, because none of the potential plant domesticates are native to the south. The wild ancestors of cereals, pulses, flax and of most of the domes-ticable animals are to be found in the foothills of the mountains surrounding the plains of north Syria and north Mesopotamia, which run down the western border of Iran. Does this perhaps suggest that these areas were the homelands of some of the earliest settlers in the south?

The settlers seem to have grown barley and a little wheat on the slopes of the turtlebacks on which they settled, and their most common domesticated animals were the pig and the cow. Sheep and goat were present, but not in any great numbers, probably because the marshy conditions did not suit them. A little later, towards the end of the fifth millennium, there is evidence for the presence of the date palm that was to become so important in the life of the early settlers. It is possible that the plant was native to the marshes, but this is unclear. Alternatively, it may originally have been imported from the shores of the Arabian Peninsula, where there is evidence for its use somewhat earlier in the millennium. It is a wonderful crop, well adapted to growing in the brackish water surrounding the settlements and, once fertilized, needing minimal care. It provided virtually the only timber easily available: its leaves were woven to provide mats and all sorts of containers, and its fruits were sweet and nutritious and could be stored for long periods. Even the date stones could be burnt to make charcoal or ground up as animal fodder.

Evidence for these early settlers was found at Ur in a series of test pits sunk by Woolley, the deepest of which was 18 metres and established the relative dating of a number of early pottery styles according to the depth at which they were found. Woolley knew from excavations at other sites such as al Ubaid, where he himself had worked, Warka/Uruk and Kish that there had been several millennia of early occupation in southern Iraq before the levels contemporary with his 'Royal Graves' of the third millennium (see Chapter 4), so the presence of these early occupation levels at Ur did not surprise him. The people of his early levels lived in small groups, in flimsy reed and mud houses, perhaps like those still used by the Marsh Arabs. There may have been more substantial buildings elsewhere in the settlement, as Woolley seems to have dug its edge. The people who lived in these huts used a distinctive type of pottery called Ubaid ware after the site where it was first found.

This pottery was largely handmade, although some of the latest examples were made on a slow wheel. The clay was often a distinctive greenish colour and decoration was added in a black or purple paint. In the early examples the decoration was tightly knit across much of the vessel and looks a little fussy to us today. Later the decoration became much simpler and bolder. The fabric varied from coarse and porous, to very fine and well fired. The shapes were usually open ones: bowls and cups predominated, but storage jars and other types of containers, usually made of the heavier fabric rather than the fine ware, were also found, especially in the later levels. Small amounts of other types of pottery also occurred. There is evidence from the sites of al Ubaid itself and from Eridu that areas at both tells were dedicated to pottery manufacture, showing clearly that, in the later part of the period at least, pottery was being manufactured on an industrial scale.

It was clear from the number of levels in Woolley's pits which contained this Ubaid pottery that the site was in use for a very long time. At Ur, the attempt to date the early levels in the pits was complicated by the fact that many of them had been badly disturbed by later levelling and quarrying for soil, so that the pottery was frequently not in its original position in the sequence of deposits. It was sometimes found mixed with far later material, sometimes on its own. Later, as more evidence was gathered, particularly from the site of Eridu, not far from Ur, this long sequence of levels was to be divided into four successive styles of pots closely related to each other, but stylistically distinct. They were initially called Eridu ware, Hajji Mohammed, and Ubaid 1 and 2 wares. This nomenclature was later changed to underline the essential continuity from one style to the next and became Ubaid 1 to 4: Eridu ware becoming Ubaid 1, and so on. More recently still, two further divisions have been added. Ubaid 0, at the beginning of the sequence, resulted from important work carried out by a French team at a site called Tell al Oueili, which had Ubaid levels below Ubaid 1. It also had a different style of pottery above Ubaid 4, this latter being called Ubaid 5. This formed a transitional level to the Uruk style of pottery that succeeded the Ubaid.

When Woolley was working at Ur in the 1930s, there was no method for giving these early levels absolute dates. Instead, they were dated relatively by their position in the sequence of stratigraphic levels. The character of each level was based on the changes in the style of pottery found in each. In south Mesopotamia the four main Ubaid levels are the earliest found so far, followed by the Uruk, the Jemdat Nasr and the Early Dynastic levels. (As we have seen, the different styles of pottery were usually called after the sites at which they were first found, so we have the Uruk style and the Jemdat Nasr type). By the Early Dynastic period the first translatable writing began to appear, mainly on clay tablets: the earliest were usually economic or administrative in nature, potentially providing another type of dating evidence. By about 2800 BC, writing was becoming more flexible and was being used for a wider range of purposes, such as the first royal inscriptions. With them came the possibility of historical or, more accurately, quasi-historical dating. Now, thanks to the sciences, a number of techniques have been developed for absolute dating, of which the most important is carbon-14 dating. This technique has allowed more precise absolute dating, although there are still some problems with its use, particularly when using samples collected many years ago for different purposes, when contamination can falsify the results. Results can also be distorted by a number of other factors such as the presence of bitumen from ancient geological deposits, which gives far too early a date. There can also be problems with the statistical margin of error, which can be large. The recent absolute dates for the Ubaid period seem to span as much as 1,500–2,000 years, from about 5800 to 4200 BC.

The findings from Woolley's pits agreed well with evidence from other Ubaid sites in south Mesopotamia and painted much the same picture (Fig. 2. i). The pottery sherds were by far the most common finds; in addition to the wares described above, there were a few sherds of burnished ware and of wares with red paint. There were also some curious pottery objects which are one of the hallmarks of the Ubaid. These are small pegs with a cup-shaped head sometimes decorated with black lines. It is difficult to know what they were intended for, but it is possible that they were supports for miniature vessels, which are also found. The peg could be set in the ground and the vessel set in the hollow in the head of the peg. Woolley thought that some of the clumsier ones had been wall

2.i Deep sounding Pit X. © British Museum, London

cones, which were used in the later Uruk period to decorate the walls of public buildings by pushing them into the clay plaster on the exterior of the building and painting or inlaying the heads in bright colours to form striking patterns.

Woolley found tools such as crude stone hoes, obsidian tools and serrated flints set in handles for cutting reeds and barley; there were also sickles made entirely out of hard-baked clay. These were surprisingly effective and were disposable, as they were so easy to replace. There were beautifully made polished stone axes, some of which are quite small. There were even clay models of axes, but it is not clear if they were actually used. It is difficult to imagine what the clay ones might have been used for – perhaps to split reeds. The presence of two types of arrowhead (triangular ones and very fine evenly flaked leaf-shaped ones) suggests that hunting may still have provided some of the protein needed by the inhabitants, although the bulk of it probably came from the abundant fish and game caught in nets, which may have been thrown or staked out in the water. Variously shaped stones may well have been used as weights for these nets, while slightly later, fish hooks and spears are also found.

The presence of clay spindle whorls indicates that textiles were already being processed, but we cannot tell if they were used to produce linen or woollen thread. The evidence from north Mesopotamia suggests that the processing of wool became increasingly important during the Ubaid period, as increasingly fine threads could be produced. One result of this advance was that sheep became more and more important to the farmer and to the economy.

It is a little surprising that there is not much evidence for any sort of personal adornment at Ur. A few beads were collected – mainly of shell or coloured stone. A number of small discs of clay or stone with flanges round the edges seem to have been inserted in ears, noses or lips, a little like the fashion for multiple piercings seen today. One disc was found close to the chin of a burial in south-west Iran, probably fallen from the lower lip, while in the Gulf they are often found in pairs, suggesting that they were worn in ears or nostrils. Some figurines from the period seem to be wearing similar discs, represented by pellets of clay stuck on to the face of the figurine. The pellets are often found on the shoulders as well, and probably indicate something different: a cape or large collar, perhaps. Tattooing or scarification has also been suggested to explain the pellets. A few small 'nails' of clay come from Ubaid sites across the south, and some of these, too, may have been decorative, while others look more like little sticks for applying kohl or other forms of face paint. Much larger ones, with a curved stalk that forms a handle, are found at a number of contemporaneous sites, and, because they show signs of wear on their heads, are generally thought to have been some sort of pestle. What they ground up is unknown, but it might have been cosmetics or herbs, or anything else available in only small quantities. They are too small to have been used for cereals.

The picture painted by the finds from Ur suggests a society with little in the way of social differentiation, probably pretty well self-sufficient, living on its own resources of fish, and herding a few animals which may have provided meat, milk and fibres for thread. There is surprisingly little in the way of imported materials or manufactured goods, apart from the pottery. There are blades made of obsidian (a volcanic glass, likely to have come from Anatolia or from western Arabia); bitumen, probably from the Hit area, was most likely used as waterproofing and as glue; and some stone axes which may be made of non-local stone; but there is little else. Much of the flint and stone used at these early Ubaid sites seems to have been brought down the Euphrates in the spring floods.

This picture of a society without sharp distinctions of wealth or status is supported by the graves found by Woolley that were all furnished in much the same way. The body was usually laid out flat on its back, sometimes on a bed of pottery sherds, and was accompanied by a variable number of pots that were probably originally full of food and drink. There was no special orientation of the body, but, interestingly, the slightly later graves from the Ubaid cemetery at Eridu were almost all laid on their backs with the heads oriented to the north-west, towards the later ziggurat, which probably had an earlier temple beneath it. It may be pushing supposition too far to suggest that the lack of a canonical orientation at Ur might mean that no shrine existed there at this early time. Even if there were one, we are unlikely to find it, as it is probably deep within the later ziggurat terrace.

A few beads and other trinkets were recovered from the graves: one had a model of an axe in clay, and a few contained clay figurines of women. The figurines show wasp-waisted women with curious snout-like faces and slits for eyes. Their heads are elongated cones, often covered with bitumen, perhaps originally intended to hold a headdress in place. They are nude with simple painted lines on them which may represent belts or jewellery, while some have pellets of clay stuck to their shoulders. Two of the ones found in graves at Ur were carrying babies in their arms, and more, without babies, were found from around the site, so they were not just gifts to the dead, but were used by the living too.

At nearby Eridu, a single male figure was found in the grave of an elderly female. He had the same snout-like face and elongated head as the females.

His shoulders were covered with pellets of clay and his hands were held close to his waist with the elbows bent, the right hand holding a stick or sceptre (?) whose other end rests on his right shoulder. The significance of these distinctive figurines is something we will, unfortunately, never know. We can only guess that they may have represented some kind of protective spirit to help the person in the grave in their afterlife (Fig. 2.ii).

Interestingly, it has recently been recognized that at some Ubaid and Ubaid-related sites in north Mesopotamia, the skulls of the dead show evidence of head-shaping, whereby the skull was artificially elongated by means of binding when a young child. There is no evidence for this from Ur because the bones were poorly preserved, and most of the skulls were already too badly broken for study. There is some inconclusive evidence for the practice from the site of Eridu, not far from Ur; however the bones need to be reassessed to confirm the presence or absence of this habit. It is possible that the curiously elongated heads of the figurines described above are an attempt to portray the results of extreme head-binding. This practice of skull-binding, where found, is usually confined to only a proportion of the burials, which seems to be a pointer to the existence of some sort of 'special' group within society. Unfortunately, there is little good-quality physical anthropological evidence from these early excavations, so other examples of the practice may not have been recognized. The pellets could represent scarification or tattooing, but, once again, the evidence is not good enough for this to be identified.

The graves from Ur may not have yielded rich finds, but they do point to one important fact about early Ubaid society: they indicate that there was some concept of an afterlife, as the dead were disposed of with care, and the pots seem to have provided the deceased with the essentials of food and drink. This belief seems to have been general, as all the burials are disposed of in broadly the same way. We shall see further evidence for this deduction when we look at the architecture from other Ubaid sites where the first temples appear during the Ubaid period.

Woolley subdivided his Ubaid graves into two groups on the basis of the depths at which they were found. The two groups were separated by a thin layer of silt. A much thicker layer of silt separated the lower graves from the remains of the village beneath, which itself had three phases, the oldest being at the ancient sea level. This silt layer, up to 3.7 metres thick, initially puzzled Woolley, but it did not take long for him to interpret it as the remains of a vast flood – in fact, of Noah's Flood. For him, here was archaeology demonstrating the literal truth of the Bible.

2.ii Ubaid figurines by Tessa Rickards

This assumption was rapidly questioned as flood levels were found at a number of other southern sites, but not all of the same date, indicating the possibility that there had been a number of localized floods rather than one huge inundation. Some sites, by contrast, showed a surprising absence of flooding. For instance, at the site of Eridu, about twelve miles south-west of Ur, no flood level was found. Other sites on the plain, as we have noted, have flood deposits at different periods. At Fara, the flood level was found above the Jemdat Nasr levels and below the level with the archaic Fara tablets, generally thought to date to the EDII/III phase. At Kish, which admittedly lies considerably further north, four flood levels were found, none as thick as the one at Ur, all lying between the Jemdat Nasr and Early Dynastic III levels. Sadly for Woolley, it seems that he was not looking at Noah's Flood. In spite of this, folk memories of exceptional flooding at a number of the most important sites in south Mesopotamia may well have played a part in the development of the famous flood story in the Gilgamesh legend, and from this to the biblical story.

The evidence from Ur is deficient in one major area. As we have seen, there were no complete structures in any of Woolley's soundings, and on the evidence they provide of wattle-and-daub huts, we might see the first settlers as poor and unsophisticated. We must not forget that these deep pits only give us a tiny window into what may already have been a large village. Certainly Ubaid pottery was found at the base of a deep sounding made in the courtyard of the later ziggurat, about 200 metres away from Woolley's pit F, suggesting that some kind of early buildings were to be found in this area too. There is also evidence for earlier Ubaid wares found in the fill of Neo-Babylonian levels. The wattle-and-daub fragments from the soundings may represent the poorer houses from the outskirts of a much larger village, while it is possible that more imposing remains lie deeply covered in the centre of the settlement. This tentative suggestion is strengthened by finds from contemporaneous sites of well-built and carefully planned buildings. In addition, the plans of major public buildings have also been found elsewhere, notably at Eridu – which, as we have seen, lies within twelve miles of Ur – so it cannot have been lack of skill that has left us with nothing more than reed huts at Ur.

There seem to be two architectural traditions for domestic architecture in the Ubaid period, the older of which is found at the site of Oueili. Here, in Ubaid 0 levels, some impressive buildings were uncovered, one measured 140 square metres. Each house appears to have had a rectangular central hall, flanked on the long sides by further rooms. The possibility of a second floor, or of access to the roof, is suggested by three narrow, parallel rooms in one corner of the building, which appear to have supported a stair. The central hall was roofed, and the roof was supported on two rows of square pillars. The excavators also claim that a standard unit of measurement of 0.58 metres was used to plan the building. (We should perhaps be a little cautious about these claims, as much of the printed plan is in fact a reconstruction.)

The second tradition is best exemplified by houses from a site called Abada, east of the Tigris in the Jebel Hamrin. Here, unusually, we have almost the whole plan of a small village. There are nine or ten houses, a workshop area, drains and storage facilities for grain. The houses are mostly freestanding and there is no sign of a defensive wall around the village, which stands on a low rise and covers an area about 170 metres by 150 metres. One house stands out by virtue of its size and the relatively rich nature of the finds. These include Ubaid 2/3 pottery, infant burials in pots below the floor, and a number of counters apparently representing an early accounting device. The house's exterior is decorated with buttresses and recesses, and it has a large yard, or terrace, to the north-east. The plan of the house is extremely ingenious, and consists of three elements, which differ in size and in the detail of their layout, neatly fitted together to form a whole. The largest unit has a T-shaped central hall and gives access to the other two units; the one to the north has a smaller version of the T-shaped hall seen in the central unit, and more rooms on either side of it, while to the south of the central hall lies the third unit, which appears to have a rectangular central hall with adjacent rooms.

The T-shaped central hall with adjacent rooms is found elsewhere in the Hamrin, over a large swathe of north Mesopotamia and in eastern Anatolia. In the Hamrin, another fine example was uncovered at Madhhur, which is dated later in the Ubaid period and where it is again clear that the central hall was roofed. In north Mesopotamia there are rather scrappy plans from sites like Tulul eth Thalathat, while at Değirmentepe, not far from Malatya in Turkey, a number of very similar units have been identified. Here they are tightly packed together, not freestanding, to form a solid mass of buildings, each of which was probably accessed from the roof. The remains of smelting in the houses show the metal was already being exploited.

These T-shaped houses are also of considerable size, some apparently measuring as much as 100 square metres, suggesting that they housed an extended rather than a nuclear family. At the moment, the examples at Abada are earlier than those at Değirmentepe, but it is too soon to say that the design originated in the Hamrin and travelled north: more evidence is needed. It is clear that the T-shaped central hall was an extremely influential design, used for both private houses and public buildings in the Ubaid, and continuing in use in the succeeding Uruk period. At the moment we do not know if this distinctive style was also used in the southern plain.

The evidence from the burials seems to point to an increasing formalization of beliefs during the Ubaid and this is supported by a series of remarkable public buildings at the site of Eridu. Seventeen levels were excavated in all, and from level 11 to level 9 there is evidence for incomplete plans of a large building standing on a platform composed of the remains of earlier levels 17 to 12. In level 8, for the first time, the plan of the whole building can be reconstructed, and there is little doubt that we are looking at a monumental temple, rebuilt on a similar plan in levels 7 and 6. It must have been an impressive building, standing proudly above the houses, and approached by a flight of stairs. Its exterior was decorated with buttresses and recesses which would have thrown a pattern of deep shadows alternating with sunshine on the otherwise undecorated outer walls. All these levels at Eridu can be attributed to the successive phases of the Ubaid period.

The plan of the central room of the temple was rectangular rather than T-shaped, and served as the sanctuary. It had an altar at one end and a large offering table close to the other. In level 6 it is estimated that this central hall measured 14.40 metres by 3.70 metres. Thick deposits of ash were found all around the offering table, and mixed in with the ash were the bones of both sea and freshwater fish. We know that in historical times the city of Eridu was thought to be the seat of Ea/Enki, the god of both fresh and salt water – so fish would have been a particularly appropriate offering. The sanctuary was flanked by smaller rooms on either side, which were probably used to store temple furniture and more offerings. One of the unusual pottery vessels used in temple 6 seems to have been a censer for burning some sort of incense, while a pottery model of a snake with a head which could be moved from side to side may have been used in some sort of divination ritual.

The only other temple in the south, of Ubaid date, was found at Uruk, lying partly below the Anu ziggurat and the Steingebaude, a mysterious building of the Uruk period. Once again, the plans are very fragmentary, but the fact that they lie beneath the younger Anu temple argues strongly for their identification as temples too. The remains of two superimposed temples were found, but it is difficult to say much about them, as so little of the plans survive. The walls that do survive are buttressed and niched, like the ones of the temples at Eridu; the remains of a stepped altar were uncovered at the north end of the central area. The excavators thought that these temples, too, had been tripartite. The evidence in the north shows that the tripartite plan had also taken root here. The best examples come from the small site of Tepe Gawra in the north-east of the country, but they are certainly not slavish copies of the southern ones and show a number of significant differences, such as deep porches protecting the entrance. There is also at least one monumental building at Gawra: the central temple of level XIII, the plan of which has no counterpart in the south at all – so the influence of the southern tradition should not be overemphasized.

One of the most fascinating aspects of the Ubaid period is the huge area over which Ubaid-related traits are found. This area can be subdivided into smaller units on various grounds, such as the type of environment and the resources available, as well as the local pottery styles, but the links between them are not easy to disentangle. When each region has a different set of resources, exchange between the regions is almost inevitable. There were inherent problems in exchange networks and we must not forget that transport was not easy over long distances 7,000 years ago; boats certainly gave easy access along the rivers, but only when travelling downstream, while on land the wheel had not yet been invented and neither the donkey nor the horse had yet been domesticated in the Fertile Crescent. Man was the major beast of burden, though cattle could drag sleds over some types of terrain. The two characteristics of the southern Ubaid which travelled furthest from home are the houses with a T-shaped central hall, found as far away as Değirmentepe in Eastern Anatolia, and various types of pottery, sometimes made on the slow wheel, with black decoration on a buff background. The clay 'pestles' with a bent haft also turn up far from south Mesopotamia.

The traditional explanations for this phenomenon were based on the assumption that southern Mesopotamia was the most advanced region in the ancient Near East and that other areas were eager to copy its achievements. However, research now indicates that, in some respects, north Mesopotamia, north Syria and parts of Anatolia were far ahead of the south; they had been using stamp seals for centuries, as a means of identification, and as an administrative tool. These are largely absent in the south; people were already adept at smelting and working copper and lead – metals which are seldom, if ever, found in the south – and their pottery was far more sophisticated than the early Ubaid wares. The Halaf wares were contemporaneous with the early Ubaid, and thus demonstrate a mastery of firing and decoration unmatchable elsewhere in the region. Perhaps, in the light of this, we should be asking why the groups in the north borrowed from the south at all?

There is one area in which the south does seem to have outstripped the north, and that is in architecture. In the north there is little evidence for the elaborate domestic houses that we find at sites such as Abada, and there are no monumental buildings like the temples from Eridu. This may in part be due to the different building materials in the two areas; mud brick is more flexible in some respects than stone, but, on the other hand, the north had access to big timbers suitable for rafters, and had mastered techniques such as vaulting that are unknown in the south at this early stage. Were architectural ideas the first to be borrowed, and often modified, followed later by other traits, such as the distinctive pottery and the clay pestles? The adoption of certain southern characteristics was a gradual process: not all southern traits were adopted at once in the north, and the pace was probably different from one region to the next.

The traditional explanations for this wide spread of similar traits are either conquest or trade. Neither is entirely satisfactory to explain the spread of Ubaid characteristics across such a vast area of the ancient Near East. It is difficult to believe that the people of the south – living in hamlets or large villages, with little evidence for social differentiation, or for the presence of large numbers of weapons – were capable of mounting military expeditions and then of maintaining their presence outside their homeland. In addition, there is little evidence for destruction levels in the north suggesting conquest. As for trade, it has already been remarked how little evidence there is for imported goods during the Ubaid in south Mesopotamia. Except for obsidian (originating in most cases from eastern Anatolia), bitumen (probably from the Hit area, which may have been available to anyone who could come and collect it), and some exotic stones and shells used for beads, there is nothing. As for the obsidian, we do not know whether it was traded 'down-the-line' – that is to say, passed hand to hand from source to destination, with the quantity diminishing at each handover – or whether people from the south travelled to its source to fetch it, or if people from the north brought it southwards. There is also the problem of what was being exported by the south in exchange for these putative trade goods.

Other mechanisms can be suggested to explain the spread of southern characteristics. For instance, as far as the Persian Gulf is concerned, it seems that the decorated pottery found there, which was made in south Mesopotamia, was regarded as a luxury and a prestige item which could open doors, but it is not clear what the travellers were taking home with them, if anything. It has been suggested that the pottery may have been given to the occupants of coastal sites like H3 in Kuwait in return for permission to pass through tribal waters and to fish there, or to replenish their water supply from local wells. This sort of mechanism may also have applied when travelling north to collect bitumen, but probably not to the acquisition of obsidian. In summary, the trade goods could be intangible and so archaeologically invisible (and thus, before the advent of writing, lost to us).

There are still more possible mechanisms by which objects and ideas can be diffused. One is by the movement of people out of their homeland, due, perhaps, to population pressures or to local environmental change. When the new land is not heavily populated this movement need not lead to conflict. Marriage between groups may also bring slow social change as ideas are imported with the incomer, whether male or female. In summary, neither warfare nor trade, in the traditional sense of the exchange of goods for 'profit', now seems to be an adequate explanation for the spread of Ubaid-related items. By contrast, there does seem to have been interaction within the different groups outside south Mesopotamia which appear to be linked by pottery styles and by exchange. As we have seen, each region had a different set of resources: there was copper in Anatolia, for example; cereals on the plains; and excellent grazing in the foothills of the mountains – a situation which encouraged exchanges between different groups.

We should, perhaps, be thinking in terms of a series of interlocking circles of people, each interacting in slightly different ways with their neighbours. These ways may have included genuine trade, the exchange of goods for other purposes, movements of people, intermarriage, and no doubt occasional raiding. Sadly, the evidence from Ur is so fragmentary that we cannot tell what its contribution to this complex system may have been.

Uruk and Jemdat Nasr Phases

The Ubaid period at Ur gave us important new evidence on burial customs and on a major inundation, while the third-millennium levels provide a mass of evidence for the 'political' importance of Ur from about 2800–2400 BC, but the evidence for the periods in between is much thinner. We have to look outside Ur to understand the Uruk and Jemdat Nasr periods. Some of the most important innovations in the history of Mesopotamia occurred in the former. The Ubaid levels at Ur are gradually replaced by those belonging to the Uruk phase. There is no evidence in the stratigraphy for violent destruction, for desertion of the site, or for another great flood. From perhaps as early as 4000 BC some major changes can be seen in the pottery recovered from the kiln stratum and the later Ubaid levels that overlay the great flood levels, which in turn lay over the earliest Ubaid remains in Pit F. The kiln stratum is so called because of the large number of pottery kilns and associated debris found in it. The discovery of an 'industrial zone' strongly suggests that this area was outside the town proper at this period, as a good deal of heat, smoke and ashes would have been generated, and there was always a danger of fire in heavily built-up areas. The greenish over-fired pottery with clumsy, painted decoration, typical of the latest Ubaid levels, is replaced with pots made on a fast wheel rather than the earlier tournette or slow wheel. In addition, the fabric is different and most of the pots are now of plain buff ware rather than the greenish ware of the late Ubaid. We also see small numbers of highly burnished vessels with a red or black finish. Others have a thin wash or slip over the surface of the vessel; this could be wiped off in part before firing, and the remaining slip burnished to create attractive shiny geometric patterns.

However, the signature pot of the period is a crude, clumsily handmade bowl with very little charm. The bowls seem to have been made by pushing the clay roughly into moulds of different sizes. Surplus clay was then cut off round the mouth of the bowl, leaving the slightly bevelled rim, which gives the bowls their name: Bevelled Rim bowls, or BRBs for short. The BRBs were obviously mass-produced in very large numbers, although, while that much is incontrovertible, there is no agreement on what they were used for. One popular idea is that they were used to distribute rations to the workers (who were dependent on the major institutions of the day, such as the temples, for their daily requirements). Each worker would have received a bowl full of grain, or perhaps of some kind of porridge. The more skilful workers would have had a larger ration in a larger bowl, women and children smaller amounts. This would explain the variable size of the BRBs. One problem with this idea is that the bowls were made and used at very small village sites as well as in towns, and it seems unlikely that there would have been representatives of 'central government' handing out rations in such small sites. Other suggestions are that they were for offerings to the gods, or that they were for baking leavened bread. The uncertainty continues, though the ration bowl theory is perhaps the most plausible and the most widely accepted.

The BRBs are found in large numbers at almost every site of Uruk date in south Mesopotamia, and at many sites beyond this core area, as far away as central Anatolia and western Iran (Map 2). The exact nature of the contacts with these distant places seems to have varied considerably depending in part on the distance from the Uruk heartland and various possibilities are discussed below. Over the last twenty years or so, archaeologists have been able to analyse the data from a large number of far-flung Uruk period sites. These have been classified into three different groups, depending on their apparent function and their distance from south Mesopotamia. By the late Uruk, all these sites seem to have been involved in a widespread trading network, which supplied the south of Sumer with the raw materials it desperately needed. In order to develop and maintain several of its major industries, such as metalworking, foreign raw materials were essential. Nor could the south produce the timber to roof its magnificent public buildings (p. 33). No doubt other finished products, such as wine, also travelled along the same routes from sites like Godin Tepe in western Iran, where the lees of wine have been identified by residue analysis in some of the Uruk-style jars found there. What is much less clear is what goods were exported in exchange.

The Euphrates is the major route connecting the south of Iraq with areas rich in stone, metals and timber, as well as providing the most important highway linking the two areas. It no surprise that a number of the sites with Uruk pottery

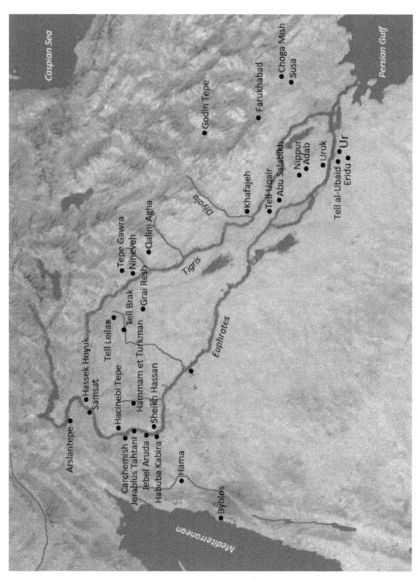

Map of Uruk trade routes © Paul Collins

and a purely southern material culture lie along its banks. The group of sites with the closest links to the south are thought to have been genuine Uruk towns founded by expatriates from the south, possibly from Uruk itself, in order to facilitate the passage of goods in both directions. A fine example of such a colony was found at a crossing on the Euphrates at a site called Habuba Kabira, close to a second site called Jebel Aruda. It seems that Habuba was built in three stages, on virgin ground, and was heavily fortified. It expanded with the arrival of each new group of colonists until, at its greatest extent, it covered 22 hectares and may eventually have housed as many as 1,500 people. Within the walls was a planned town with houses, gardens, work areas and an acropolis with monumental architecture that uses the tripartite plans familiar from the Ubaid, as do some of the houses. The workshop areas have produced evidence for the working of both silver and lead, as well as for producing pottery. There is hardly any local pottery, but classic Uruk wares are the norm. There is also a harbour on the river where boats from Anatolia, probably loaded with timber or metals such as copper and lead, could stop for supplies or unload some of their cargo. No doubt the town also forced them to pay a hefty tax. Jebel Aruda stands nearby on a bluff high above the river. It is not fortified, but the high cliffs may have given it sufficient protection. Here, there are some large houses with evidence for farming, and a large and impressive acropolis, but, overall, it is much smaller than Habuba. Both sites have produced many examples of the seals which formed the backbone of the administrative system here, as in the south.

Further away from home, there were also what are referred to in the literature as way stations, the ancient equivalents of motorway service stations with Travel Lodges, on the river: small isolated sites with a mixture of Uruk pottery and local wares. One of the best excavated is called Hassek Hüyük, in Anatolia, not far from the modern Turkish/Syrian border. The site was again fortified, but seems to have had few permanent inhabitants, as there is little in the way of accommodation. There is a large tripartite house or shrine, elaborately adorned with the clay cones that are such a typical method of decorating important buildings in the south (p. 37). There are also a number of two-dimensional terracotta animal figures, which seem to have formed part of friezes on the walls. The inhabitants here had much closer relationships with the local people than at Habuba Kabira, and the pottery shows a mixture of local north Syrian and southern Uruk characteristics. The presence of drying racks for crops, inside the fortified enclave, suggests that the people who lived there may have farmed the land immediately around the site, as well as looking after long-distance travellers.

Finally, even further away, enclaves in local towns seem to have housed people from the south whose business it was to facilitate the exchange system between the two areas. At Hacinebi, which is on a crossing place over the Euphrates in south-east Anatolia, north of Birecik, one area of the 3.3-hectare site was very different from the rest of the site: its pottery, its accounting devices, the types of animal kept and the food eaten were all related to southern sites rather than to the local ones. It is suggested that this is where the Uruk merchants lived and that, as far as possible, they used the materials and customs they were familiar with at home, rather than the local ones. Another fine example of a foreign colony was found in western Iran, on a crucial pass from Mesopotamia on to the Iranian plateau, at a place called Godin Tepe. Here, a fortified building seems to have housed merchants in the centre of a local settlement. Close comparison between the seals (p. 36) from Godin with those from Uruk and Susa suggest that the merchants here were not from Mesopotamia, but from Susa in south-western Iran. Susa, the largest town in its immediate area, seems to have had a similar network of trading centres to that in south Mesopotamia, though perhaps on a smaller scale, as the Susa region is much closer to the sources of essential raw materials.

The elaborate trading systems implied by the evidence quoted above, and the increasing complexity of urban life throughout the region, required, for the first time in history, a way of recording decisions and transactions that were too numerous or too complex to be carried in one person's head. This increased complexity, coupled with the expansion in size of urban settlements, also led to the need for a more formal structure of governance if the settlements were to function efficiently. This seems to have been true both in the large southern settlements of Mesopotamia and in south-west Iran (see Map 2).

There is relatively little evidence for the relationship between Uruk and the south-west of Iran, so it is not clear if Susa was an independent city operating its own trade network, or was tied to Uruk in some way and was operating on its behalf. Certainly, there are many similarities in the material culture, but, sadly, there is little evidence for systems of government in either place. Almost the only evidence comes from pictorial representations on cylinder seals – small cylindrical pieces of stone engraved with a variety of scenes, which came into use in the middle of the Uruk period at both places. These suggest that a single man wielded supreme power over the military and religious spheres in both centres. The man is depicted on the seals destroying his enemies and worshipping the gods. In spite of this evidence for warfare, it is a little difficult to believe that any city had the means of subordinating another for a considerable period, when systems of government were still rudimentary, and there is no evidence for a standing army.

Cylinder seals were not only often beautiful to look at, but also served many practical purposes, giving us an insight into the internal organization of these large towns. They could be used to establish identity or ownership by rolling them over containers of goods or even over doors 'locked' with a peg and a handful of mud; they acted as symbols of office and as authentication of authority. Not all their uses were so practical; in some cases where they apparently belonged to children, they seem to have been worn as charms against evil, or as good luck tokens. The subject matter and style of these seals changes through time, and from one area to another, so that they can also be used to establish a relative dating sequence, and often demonstrate contact between far-distant places. For example, at Hacinebi, some of the seals are local and some had their closest parallels with examples found at Uruk, while another group seems to be closer to seals from Susa, suggesting that Hacinebi was in contact with both these places. The same types of comparison suggest that the merchants from Godin may have come from Susa rather than Uruk.

A second source of information is provided by one of the most important innovations of the fourth millennium BC: the appearance of the first writing. The first attempts to convey information by this method were made by drawing simple pictures and symbols for numbers on a clay tablet with the point of a stylus. Almost all these early tablets, which are very difficult to translate as they are often mnemonic, seem to be severely practical, conveying information about goods and people working for the temple, or perhaps the palace. They have no grammar and the signs are pictographic representations of the objects/people being listed, not an attempt to reproduce speech. The system seems to have developed from earlier, simpler devices such as tokens representing different goods, which could then be grouped together and enclosed in cylindrical balls or bullae, to represent a single transaction (Fig. 3.i). These balls were then 'signed' with the cylinder seal of the relevant official, or sometimes signed and countersigned, which indicates the development of an increasingly complex bureaucracy. By the end of the fourth millennium BC, the system had become far more sophisticated. The scribes were able to attribute sounds to the symbols as well as their pictographic meaning. This allowed them to build up more complex words and personal or place names, thereby conveying far more information. The range of subject matter also began to expand beyond the economic, and for the first time we find a list of professions, grouped in a hierarchy, with the most important member of each group listed first. This is a much-copied text, and the later copies, which are easier to read, have a word that can be translated as king at the top. Each group of specialists also begins with someone called the chief butcher, baker or candlestick maker, strongly suggesting that society as a whole was organized in a hierarchical way, with a king or similar authority figure at the top of the pyramid.

Sadly, very few of these important developments are to be seen in the Uruk-period evidence from Ur. However, Woolley excavated a number of Uruk-period graves, which were dug into the industrial debris from a large number of pottery kilns. They showed clear differences from those of the earlier period. Instead of being laid full-length on their backs, the dead were buried on their sides with their knees flexed in a position suggestive of sleep. It is tempting to see this change in position as indicating a change in religious beliefs, but it was very gradual and does not seem to have been accompanied by a change in the plan of temple buildings, which might be expected in the case of a fundamental change in beliefs. Instead, there is obvious continuity in plans, similar to those from Eridu (see Chapter 2). Sadly, we have to accept that this interesting problem cannot be solved on the evidence currently available.

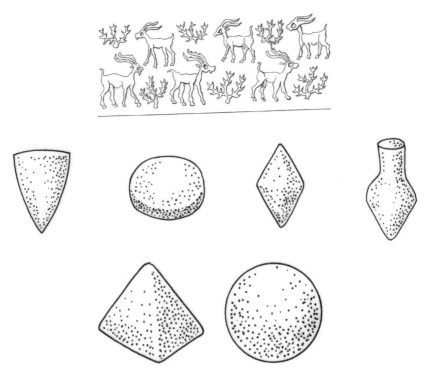

3.i Cylinder seal and counters by Tessa Rickards

The contents of the graves were also different. A much wider range of objects is now found, and instead of pottery alone, as in the Ubaid graves, there is now an emphasis on vessels made of stone from a wide variety of sources outside south Mesopotamia. Some finished bowls and the unworked stones travelled down the trade routes from the Anatolian highlands and Iran, although many of the bowls were probably made in Mesopotamia itself to suit local tastes. The stones may well have travelled from their source via the network of outposts and colonies described above. There is no evidence in the Ur graves for big differences in wealth or status, though the elite may simply have been buried in another part of the site. The contemporaneous graves from Susa, on the other hand, certainly indicate the existence of an elite group that was buried with rich burial goods, including a wealth of copper artefacts, something not yet found anywhere in south Mesopotamia. It is important, when making generalizations of this sort, to remember the very partial nature of our evidence and the fact that very few graves of the period have been excavated apart from the ones at Ur. This may have distorted our picture of the nature of society.

As in the Ubaid levels at Ur, there is a lack of evidence for buildings in the Uruk period too. The only exception comprises some fragmentary remains found below the equally tantalizingly incomplete remains of the Early Dynastic period, below a corner of the great Ur III ziggurat. Once again, we have to look elsewhere to get an idea of the characteristic monumental buildings of the Uruk period. We have already seen that at Habuba Kabira and Jebel Aruda some buildings stood out because of their size and their position on a raised 'acropolis'. In south Mesopotamia the most remarkable group of public buildings comes from the great site of Uruk/Warka, north of Ur, on the other side of the Euphrates. Here, by the middle of the fourth millennium BC, two enclaves of public buildings were built on a monumental scale, representative of a huge investment of time and expense. This amount of investment must indicate how important the edifices were to the community. There are important differences between the two centres: the one known as Kullaba or the Anu ziggurat, as its name suggests (the word ziggurat comes from the Assyrian for 'raised up'), stood high above the town with a single temple on top. In reality, it is not a true stepped ziggurat like those found from the third millennium BC onwards, but a high terrace, which almost certainly encloses earlier temples. The second group of buildings, the Eanna complex, is not built on a high terrace. It consists of a number of public buildings enclosed in a perimeter wall. The precise nature of all these buildings is not clear, and the former assumption that they were all temples seems unlikely to be true. They appear from their plans to have had a variety of functions, but the building on top of the Anu ziggurat, known as the White Temple, retains the best claim to be a genuine temple. It has the classic tripartite plan, first found in the Ubaid period, with an altar, a plinth perhaps for a statue, and an offering place in the large central space. Its external walls were originally covered with a lime wash, which must have made them gleam. This, coupled with the height of the platform, would have made the building stand out for miles around. At ground level on the north-east side of the terrace was a second even larger and rather mysterious building: its plan consists of three rectangular enclosures nesting one inside the other. There is no clue as to its purpose, although it has been suggested that it might have been some kind of cenotaph.

The Eanna complex was rebuilt a number of times during the fourth millennium. Then, at the end of the Uruk period, all the structures were knocked down and a large area flattened to form a base housing a number of different structures, of which only tiny fragments survive. This huge clearance meant that, sadly, very few objects originally used in the buildings were retrieved and the plans of the destroyed buildings were not always easy to recon-struct, as, in most cases, only the stubs of the walls survive. The earliest building in the complex, dating to Uruk level V, was the Stone Cone Mosaic building. It stood in its own enclosure in the north-west corner of the perimeter wall. Its walls had been lavishly decorated with cones of stone inserted into the walls, the contrasting colours of the stone making striking geometric patterns. Many of the other later buildings were decorated in much the same way, although the cones used were usually of clay with painted heads rather than of stone.

Another building of approximately the same date at Uruk lies to the south-east in its own enclosure and is called the Limestone Temple, as it is built of poor-quality local limestone. It is a very large tripartite temple measuring 27 metres by 80 metres. Its plan is fragmentary, but it looks as if it had a T-shaped central area like the Ubaid house at Abada, for instance. Once again, this stresses the continuity between the two periods. Above the Cone Mosaic temple, and built after it had gone out of use, is an odd building constructed of bricks, which may belong to the beginning of the succeeding Jemdat Nasr period. It looks as if the building were ceremonially set on fire to cremate a large number of objects (possibly furnishings of the temple below, or perhaps donations origi-nally lodged in its treasury).

In the succeeding Uruk-date periods, the plan of the enclave alters consid-erably. In level IVb, for instance, there are three platforms: two supported buildings (entered from a central courtyard), and the third supported four pairs of huge freestanding pillars. This must have given access to yet another temple, of which hardly anything remains. The platform on which the pillars stand was approached by a double staircase in the centre and a second single set of stairs at one end, against the courtyard wall, with decorative engaged half-columns. The freestanding and the engaged pillars, as well as the walls of the courtyard, were beautifully decorated with intricate cone mosaics in red, white and black. They must have formed a dazzling ensemble. Cones like this, lying loose in the soil, suggest the presence of a public building at Ur near the later ziggurat. The photograph on page 38 of *Ur of the Chaldees* also seems to show the remains of a large pillar associated with the cones, although this is barely mentioned in the text.

In the final Uruk level, IVa, there is another complete change, with the older buildings being enclosed in a massive new compound containing at least two temples. One of these, temple C, shows an interesting fusion of the tripartite plan and the T-shaped central hall as the temple divides into two interconnecting sections at right angles to one another. The 'head' is tripartite in plan, while the 'body' has a T-shaped central area. In addition, it has a number of very distinctive hearths in the central area: each looks a bit like a frying pan with a round head and a long handle at right angles to the head. Exactly the same type of hearth is found at Habuba Kabira, discussed above. There are also a number of other monumental buildings including a large empty space surrounded by its own wall. It has been suggested that this may have been a garden, or perhaps an enclosure built to house animals before sacrifice. A square structure with elaborately niched and buttressed walls and a large courtyard in the centre was thought by the excavators to have been a palace, but is more likely to have housed offices or stores. The structure was built over before the end of IVb and another temple, temple D, erected over it. There is also a barrel-vaulted hall and another pillared hall: both may have been meeting places. As so few artefacts were found in their original positions (except for a group of seven tablets from temple C), it is very difficult to know the buildings' true functions. Today, archaeologists are moving away from the tendency to call any building that is larger and better built than its neighbours a temple, and are considering other identifications, such as offices, stores, schools, law courts, official residences and meeting places.

Whatever the true functions of the buildings of the Eanna complex, there is no doubt that Uruk was a rich and thriving city by the end of the Uruk period. It covered an area of about 2.5 square kilometres and probably included gardens and a port on the river as well as workshops and domestic housing. It may have had 20,000 or so inhabitants, but little is known of the housing of the period, as excavation has been concentrated on the two public areas of Eanna and the Anu (Kullaba) ziggurat. Various workshop areas have been identified by survey, and found to have been working exotic stones, such as carnelian, imported from overseas. This indicates that the northern route along the Euphrates was not the only important trade route at this early period. It is always difficult to estimate past populations, but it is clear that a very large workforce would have been needed to carry out the massive building programmes seen in Eanna and Kullaba. Not all the workers needed to have been inhabitants of the city; some may have been brought in from the countryside, while others may have been captives brought in by raiding parties. There must also have been a considerable investment of resources, not only human, but also in the planning and laying out of the buildings. Timber for building had to be brought in from foreign parts, and a massive catering operation organized to feed the workers. The rapid development of recording systems and of a professional bureaucracy during the Uruk period must surely be related to the logistics of such huge public works.

With all this magnificence at Uruk, it has to be admitted that the evidence from Ur is pathetic by comparison. And yet very few, if any, burials were found at Uruk, probably because people were not buried in the great public areas of the city – so the Ur evidence does add something, however mundane, to what is known from other excavations. Together, all this evidence helps us to edge closer to a realistic picture of the Uruk period, which is one of the most exciting and innovative in the history of Mesopotamia. Scholars still discuss with passion the reasons for this extraordinary burst of creativity, which included the development of urban centres, complex societies and, most importantly of all, recording techniques (including counters, seals and the earliest attempts at writing). A new profession was developed to manage these large and internally varied towns and cities, and we see the emergence of the earliest civil servants. There were also technological innovations such as the potter's wheel and an increasing proficiency in metallurgy.

Southern Mesopotamia, exceptionally rarely in the ancient Near East, was able to produce a surplus of food and other basic commodities without major effort, as the marshes provided almost everything necessary for survival. By the Uruk period, mere survival was no longer enough, and for the material culture to develop further it was essential to import raw materials, which were lacking in the south. Perhaps the most important commodity was strong timber to roof the magnificent public buildings being erected at Uruk and other contemporaneous sites. High-quality stone was also needed for bowls, cups, plaques or statues, while decorative semi-precious stones were increasingly sought after by the emerging elite for their own adornment. As Algaze has already suggested (see further reading for this chapter), a readily available surplus in essentials and a total lack of quality raw materials seem to have been the two factors that combined to start the complex process towards the first cities.

The end of the Uruk period, about 3200 BC, seems to have been marked by retrenchment in Mesopotamia; for example, the major Uruk 'colonies' were destroyed or deserted. This must have disrupted the flow of materials to the south and limited their prosperity. At Uruk, the whole of the Eanna precinct was cleared, and a new platform made. Whether the late Uruk buildings were destroyed by enemy action or merely levelled so that new, more elaborate structures could be erected we shall never know.

There are also signs of change in the settlement pattern with a number of small sites being abandoned and new ones founded. However, at Ur there is no sign of a major disruption in the long sequence of levels from the amazingly prolific Pit F. The contents of the graves from the thick kiln levels, all of which apparently date to the Uruk period, change gradually, with the wares typical of the Uruk period giving way over time to new types more at home in the succeeding Jemdat Nasr period. A number of Jemdat Nasr graves are also found in Pits X and W, while a few more were in Pit Y. All these pits lay close together south-east of Pit F and suggest that this part of the site remained outside the settled area. The bodies in these graves lie on their sides again, but are more tightly flexed. The most distinctive pottery of the so-called Jemdat Nasr period is brightly painted in plum red, white and black, often decorating small jars with a flattened rim. Woolley also noted that there is much more metal in these upper graves, with simple bowls of lead and copper becoming commonplace and sometimes replacing the stone pots of the earlier period. Finely carved stonework continues to be found and includes bowls decorated in high relief (Fig. 3.ii), and the splendid figure of a crouching boar.

There is not much precious metal: little gold was found and silver is represented by a single pair of silver earrings. Semi-precious beads of carnelian and agate become common, and lapis lazuli from Badakshan is found as well. This distinctive stone is sometimes used for beads and sometimes as inlay.

The remains of at least three levels of houses, F, G and H, with a narrow lane separating them, were found above the kiln stratum and the Jemdat Nasr in Pit F. Level F was destroyed and level E above it probably belongs to the Early Dynastic period, though the lane remains in the same position, indicating some continuity. These houses suggest that the town was expanding out over the kiln stratum containing the graves. Interestingly, in Pit W, to the south-east of Pit

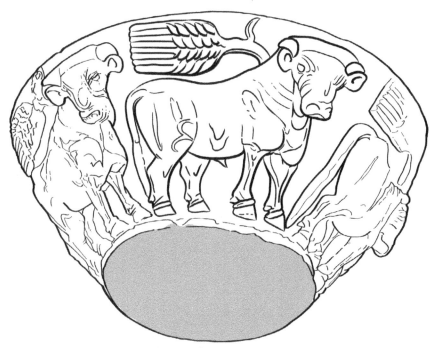

3.ii Stone Bowl with bulls from Ur by Mary Shepperson

F, a rubbish level known as SIS 6/7, which lay above most of the Jemdat Nasr graves, produced large numbers of seal impressions. These seem to have been thrown away when parcels and packages were opened nearby, perhaps in the precincts of a major public building. The level lies on a steep slope, suggesting that rubbish was thrown out over the edge of the inhabited area, which, as seen above, had now expanded beyond Pit F. At a guess, the limits of the town lay precisely here, between Pits F and W. The styles of these sealings indicate that some of them belong to the succeeding Early Dynastic I period, but others are earlier and offer a stylistic bridge between the Uruk seals and those of the Early Dynastic period. There is nothing as fine as the best of the Uruk seals, and some of the Jemdat Nasr examples are crude and schematic, but some of the motifs first seen in the Uruk, such as animal files, continue, while others, like a simple banquet scene, are elaborated into the third millennium. One distinctive group of seals known as the City Seals will be more fully discussed later.

The evidence from Uruk and Jemdat Nasr levels at Ur gives little indication of the achievements of the Uruk period, which are so impressively visible at Uruk and in the colony sites. There is no evidence for writing, for instance, and no direct evidence for monumental building, though there is indirect evidence from the graves for the importing of increasingly large amounts of foreign raw

materials – and, as we have seen, it is the only site in southern Mesopotamia
with substantial evidence for burial customs. This reflects the situation noted in
Chapter 2 for the Ubaid period and warns us again about the dangers of trying
to reconstruct the history of an area from one site alone. It is essential to draw
the scraps of evidence from as wide a range of sources as possible if we are to
put together a defensible view of the past.

4

The Rise of the City State

The Jemdat Nasr period seems to have come to an end around 2800 BC or a little earlier, and during the rest of the third millennium Ur flourished as never before. The identification of objects inscribed with the names of the rulers of the city, and with the name of the city itself, allows us to say that Ur emerged into a historical era for the first time by the middle of the third millennium. (This is perhaps a rather grandiose claim and it might be more accurate to call it a quasi-historical era.) As we shall see, the surviving sources are all rather problematical and convey little reliable historical information. In spite of this, by combining the archaeological evidence with the iconography and the written sources, we can trace the rise of Ur from a city state in about 2700 BC to the capital of what is sometimes called the world's first empire by about 2150 BC. Before the end of the third millenium, this 'empire' fell apart for reasons that are still not fully understood, and Ur never again reached such political heights.

The first quasi-historical evidence comes from a number of impressions made by cylinder seals* on clay found at Ur in the rubbish levels overlying the Jemdat Nasr cemetery. Woolley called the levels Seal Impression Strata (SIS) and the earliest strata with the earliest impressions are known as SIS8/5. The backs of the impressions show that most of them came from containers or from simple door locks. Similar impressions were found at a large number of other sites, including Jemdat Nasr itself, where they were also found on clay tablets. There are many impressions of different styles of seal from these levels, almost all dating to the first quarter of the third millennium, but one group stands out. The motifs on this group are semi-pictographic and match groups of symbols found on some very

---

* A cylinder seal is a cylinder, often of stone, usually under four centimeters long, and pierced for suspension. It is engraved with scenes and inscriptions written in reverse. When these seals are rolled on soft clay the inscription appears correctly oriented, and the design, with or without an inscription, serves as a 'signature'.

early clay tablets with lists of the names of towns on them. These lists continued to be copied for hundreds of years as part of the school curriculum, and the earliest examples can be translated by working backwards from the later versions on which the cuneiform had evolved sufficiently to be readable. By analogy, it is then also possible to translate at least some of the groups of symbols on the seal impressions that seem to have been the precursors of proper cuneiform signs. It is striking that the same groups of symbols crop up in a number of different impressions from several different cities, and give them their name of city sealings (Fig. 4.i). Not only that, but in the designs the names of four cities can be identified, and these occur in much the same order again and again. These cities are Ur, Larsa, Nippur and Uruk. The other names are less easy to identify but probably include Kesh and Zabalam, while three more remain unidentified. It seems reasonable to suggest that the most frequently appearing names had some special significance.

It appears that this group of towns was coming together for some specific purpose(s) and two possibilities have been suggested. The first is some kind of defence pact whereby cities pledged to help their neighbours in the event of an attack. The second is that these cities joined together to help supply Nippur, the religious capital, with small quantities of luxury goods such as dried fruits. They also supplied small quantities of textiles. The low numbers mentioned suggest that these were probably offerings to the holy city rather than taxes or trade goods. This second interpretation seems more convincing, and Ur's presence on these lists shows that it was already a politically significant settlement by the early third millennium BC.

More conventional historical sources begin to appear well before the middle of the third millennium. The major written sources for the reconstruction of the earliest history of south Mesopotamia include the inscriptions of the rulers themselves, often on objects dedicated to the gods by the ruler in question. Other dedications are made by women or high-ranking officials 'for the life of the ruler so and so'. Foundation deposits found in great public buildings such as palaces and temples are frequently inscribed with the name of the builder. Also so inscribed are monumental stelae commemorating major events, and stone plaques showing the ruler (and sometimes his immediate family) carrying out

4.i City sealing symbols for Ur at right-hand end by Mary Shepperson and by kind permission of Roger Matthews

his royal duties. In these types of inscription, the best possible gloss is put on the achievements of the ruler in order to impress the gods to whom the building or artefact is dedicated and ensure their approval and support. In some cases, the stelae may have been publicly displayed so that the populace, too, could be suitably impressed by their ruler's achievements and divine connections. It was probably thought that this would discourage them from revolt against a powerful and just ruler who had the protection of the gods. Each battle mentioned is a victory and every building project a lavish achievement surpassing those of earlier kings; raids into neighbouring countries are presented as conquests; trade goods from another region may be presented as tribute. It is important to remember who the audience for these inscriptions was and what the inscriptions were intended to achieve when trying to assess their historical worth. Unless there is corroboration from another source for the claims they make, it is often wise to take some of them with a pinch of salt, while some really belong in the realm of myth. Propaganda was already a well-established tool!

Administrative tablets occur from the beginning of the third millennium onwards at a number of sites on the southern plain, and are in the tradition of those found in the Uruk period. They become much more numerous, and more comprehensible, in the last quarter of the millennium, when they are found in their thousands and give a unique view of the workings of the rather bloated bureaucracy that existed under the kings of the 'imperial' Third Dynasty of Ur. In addition, we begin to find myths, poems and a number of miscellaneous texts, apparently used as exercises in the scribal schools that trained up the civil servants of the day. Lists such as the one mentioned above contained names of towns and cities, or of objects such as plants. They might almost be called specialized dictionaries or thesauruses, which group together all the words for different kinds of wood, for example, or for the different professions. This last list is especially interesting, as the first example is found in the Uruk period, and the text continues almost unchanged for generations. The legible later texts demonstrate that the list is arranged hierarchically, with the king or lord as the first entry. Each group of specialists is then grouped under its own headman or leader. The titles of some of the leaders suggest that there was also an assembly of citizens who had certain judicial and administrative responsibilities: thus we have a glimpse of the social organization of the time the text was written.

One remarkable text, known as the Sumerian King List, is available in several versions, all incomplete. It purports to be a list of all the rulers of south Mesopotamia from the earliest days 'before the flood' to the early second millennium BC, when it was written. The list also contains brief information about some of the rulers, such as the names of their fathers. Regrettably, its historicity is uncertain, and some would go further and see it as pure fiction. It was written more than a millennium after the earliest events it purports to record, and many of the early kings who ruled before the flood, and a few who came after it, are given ridiculously long reigns thus immediately raising question marks in our minds. It was also apparently written as a piece of propaganda for a dynasty of Isin, which had usurped the throne of that city in the early second millennium, and was trying to prove its legitimacy by setting itself in the venerable tradition of the King List. Such a blatant use of propaganda is another reason for caution. There are also difficulties with the fact that some rulers who are known from their own inscriptions are not mentioned in the list. For example, the so-called Ur-Nanshe Dynasty of Lagash, whose own inscriptions prove that they ruled that city for nine generations from the middle of the third millennium, is left out. The most likely explanation for this omission seems to be that Isin, where the list was written, was engaged in feuding with Lagash, and wished to discredit the latter's claim to have ruled so successfully.

Yet another problem arises from the fact that rulers of different cities, whom we know from their own inscriptions to have been contemporaries, are shown as sequential in the King List. By the middle of the third millennium, tradition insisted that kingship – which, according to the list, had come down from heaven as a gift to humankind from the gods – could only be held by one city at a time. This meant that only one city could rule over the land of Sumer at a time. Because of this belief, contemporary rulers of the city states of the plain had to be shown as following one another in order to conform to tradition. The gods had also decreed that no city could rule for ever, so that no dynasty could rule for ever either, and kingship would inevitably pass from one city to another. The end of each dynasty is recorded in the King List with the formula: 'The city X was smitten by arms and the kingship was taken to city Y.' Given all these problems, it is not difficult to see why an uncritical acceptance of the evidence of the King List, however tempting, would be likely to result in serious distortions of history.

On the basis of the archaeology of an area well to the north-east of Ur, in the Diyala valley, the third millennium is divided into the following periods: Early Dynastic I (closely allied to the preceding Jemdat Nasr period and which comes to an end about 2800 BC), Early Dynastic II (poorly defined at Ur, but distinguishable in the Diyala region) and Early Dynastic III. The latter probably began about 2600 BC, and more recently has been subdivided into two phases known as EDIIIa and IIIb, each lasting around a 100 years. By the middle of the third millennium, in EDIIIa/b, the evidence allows us for the first time to match the archaeological evidence from Ur with the evidence of the King List. The King List states that Mesannepadda was the first king of the First Dynasty of Ur, and his son Aannepadda was the second. The names of these two kings have been found on seals and sealings from the level covering the remains of the so-called royal tombs, which must therefore predate them. In absolute terms, the royal graves probably embrace the period about 2600–2450 BC, the EDIIIa period, while the seals and other material from the level overlying them belong to EDIIIb. These seals, from the level above the royal tombs, together with other inscriptions, prove the actual existence of the kings Mesannepadda and Aannepadda. Unfortunately, this raises new problems, because there are several names found on objects buried in the royal tombs below this. These must refer to earlier rulers who do not appear anywhere on the King List. One of the earliest of these may be Meskalamdug, who is given the title of *Lugal* or king. His seal was found in a box interred with a subsidiary burial in the shaft of RG 1054. Inscriptions of Ninbanda, 'the queen', have also been found on gold artefacts from the tomb, and she may have been his wife. He is probably the father of Akalamdug, who also ruled at Ur, and of Mesannepadda, the official founder of the First Dynasty of Ur who also called himself King of Kish – a title apparently implying that his sway spread well beyond Ur itself.

The richest female royal grave found by Woolley is identified by the inscriptions on the seals belonging to the main burial as that of a woman called Puabi, who carries the ambiguous title of *Nin* – it can mean queen, but also equates to the title 'Lady' (Fig. 4.ii). The lady was buried with a magnificent array of jewellery, including a great mantilla-like comb of gold topped with gold flowers, huge boat-shaped gold earrings and a cape of multicoloured beads. If we accept Puabi as a queen, then we have to ask if she was a ruler in her own right or, like Ninbanda, a spouse, or even perhaps a queen mother? (Perhaps we should also ask the same questions about Ninbanda?) There is sadly no conclusive evidence either way, although one female ruler of approximately this period is listed in the King List as having reigned in Kish. A seal with the name Abargi on it was found loose in the pit of Puabi's tomb, and it has been suggested that he could have been her husband, who was perhaps buried in the adjacent RG1789 where the main burial is thought to have been male, but this charming picture is highly speculative.

There is also at least one additional royal grave, RG1054, where the main burial appears to be female, and others where the gender is contested. Unfortunately, the bones from the cemetery were rarely preserved and were often in such a

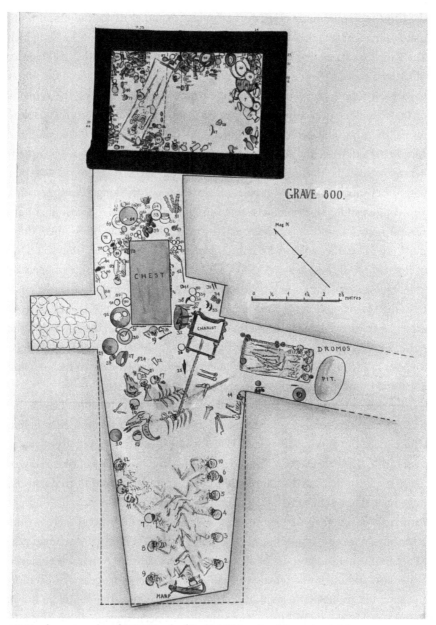

4.ii Royal cemetery plan of RG800 tomb of Puabi © University of Pennsylvania Museum

parlous state that it was not practicable to lift and store them, or to examine them forensically. One exception to this is the skeleton of Puabi. A distinguished medical man, Sir Arthur Keith, examined the bones and reported that they were of a woman, apparently in her forties. The lack of physical evidence has led scholars over the years to attempt to sex the bodies by the artefacts associated with them. The problem is that modern perceptions of female/male activities will inevitably influence the attributions; for example, the tomb of Puabi, the lady, included a gold saw and chisel, tools usually associated with a male, while the main female burial in RG1054 had a dagger at the waist and a whetstone, all finds which also suggest masculinity.

All we can say with certainty is that objects belonging to the first two rulers of the First Dynasty of Ur, as shown on the King List, were found in a level of rubbish, which covered another group of graves containing objects inscribed with at least four more royal names: two male and two female. All these were previously unknown and must predate the First Dynasty. There were also a number of other personal names, which may have been those of royalty, but they were not accompanied by the designation 'king' or 'queen'.

By the EDIII period, the city of Ur covered about fifty hectares. The inscriptions came from a cemetery south-east of the later ziggurat and partly below the wall that encloses the sacred area, or *temenos*, built by Nebuchadnezzar in the first millennium BC. This enclosed a much larger area than that of the earlier sacred precinct. It seems that rubbish from the early buildings within the smaller precinct was thrown out over the wall, and formed the Seal Impression Strata mentioned earlier. Up to 2,000 graves were dug into it. In the lower EDIIIa cemetery, a smaller group of just sixteen graves was clustered together in the heart of the cemetery area. They were distinguished by a number of characteristics. When the tomb was undisturbed, the body in the main burial wore sumptuous finery and was placed in a tomb chamber at the bottom of a deep shaft, and oriented to the points of the compass. It was accompanied by extremely rich burial goods and by a variable number of other people who may have been members of the court. In some cases, there were only five or six, but in one case there were up to seventy-five, most of them richly dressed. There were also soldiers with their armour and weapons, musicians with their instruments, and baggage wagons drawn by oxen (p. 50).

The shafts of these tombs were covered by a largely unbroken grey layer of rubbish called SIS I/II, but it is no longer possible to establish with certainty the level from which the shafts were originally dug, as erosion has destroyed the evidence. It has also made it impossible to say if some kind of monument or shrine was originally erected over the shafts. Woolley thought there were traces of such structures, and considerable evidence exists for post-burial rituals, including offerings of food and drink. This suggestion is supported by inscriptions from the contemporary site of Lagash. It has been suggested by a more recent study that the area was deliberately levelled before the graves were dug to provide a large, flat space as close as possible to the sacred precinct. Here, the elaborate burial rites could be seen by large numbers of people not directly involved in the ceremonies. In SISI/II were the seals of the First Dynasty kings of EDIIIb, Mesannepadda and Aannepadda. Above this again were later graves dating to the last quarter of the third millennium BC. Because the rubbish layers lay at a steep angle to the presumed early third-millennium wall, the absolute depth of the graves told Woolley little about the relative dates of the 2,000 or so burials. By following the tip lines and through the sequence-dating of pots and stone vessels he was able to group the graves together according to age.

The uncovering of the royal graves at Ur sealed Woolley's reputation as one of the greatest archaeologists of the twentieth century, and one of the luckiest. He displayed enormous skill, imagination and energy in retrieving and restoring some of the most beautiful objects ever found in Mesopotamia, as well as remarkable self-control. In 1922 one of the first trial trenches at the site started to uncover a large number of small gold beads and Woolley quickly realized that this was evidence for what promised to be a rich cemetery. He felt that his workers were not yet sufficiently skilled to tackle what was going to be the arduous and delicate job of excavating large numbers of important burials. He redeployed them to other parts of the site until 1927, almost five years later, when he judged them sufficiently well trained to begin work on the cemetery again. He was to find as many as 2,000 graves, the bulk of which covered a period of perhaps 300 years, from EDIIIa to the end of the succeeding Agade period. There were also some later burials. The majority of graves were those of private individuals buried in simple coffins or wrapped in reed mats in pits in the ground, but sixteen graves stood out because of both their construction and their contents.

These burials lay close together at the heart of the cemetery, usually in stone-built chambers at the bottom of deep shafts. They were approached by a sloping ramp, or occasionally by steps. In front of the tomb chamber was an open space where grave goods were deposited. The grave goods were of a staggering richness and variety, but the outstanding feature was the presence of what appeared to be human sacrifices, sometimes just two or three, but sometimes up to eighty. A number of inscribed objects in the graves displayed personal names with the designation 'king', as discussed above. These inscriptions, together with the stone chambers and the rich contents, persuaded Woolley that the sixteen graves should be considered as those of the early rulers of Ur, even though their names did not appear in the King List. (In the excavation reports, the 'royal' graves were usually designated RG and the others PG or private graves, but the denominations are not entirely consistent.)

Grave PG755 is difficult to classify. Instead of having a built, stone chamber, a wooden coffin lay at the bottom of a deep shaft. It had very rich grave goods, but no human sacrifice. The grave was dug down into the shaft of RG779, the so-called king's grave. In the coffin was the body of a young man and a number of gold objects with the name Meskalamdug on them. The inscriptions did not carry the designation 'king', unlike the cylinder seal found above RG1054. This suggests that the young man may have been a member of the ruling dynasty, named after the king, but not a king himself. He was perhaps a prince and a soldier, to judge from the magnificent gold parade helmet found next to the body, and the fine weapons inside and outside the coffin, which may have belonged to him in life. It is notable that some rich female jewellery was also found in the coffin. Outside it were many weapons, including spears placed upright against the wall of the shaft. Woolley, however, decided that the lack of associated sacrificial burials probably meant PG755 was not strictly a royal burial, in spite of its riches.

The construction techniques used for the stone and brick tombs were of an unsuspected sophistication and Woolley saw them as rewriting the history of architecture. Some of the burial chambers comprised up to four chambers placed at the bottom of the grave shaft and almost all were made of rough limestone or of a mixture of stone and mud brick. There is an outcrop of this stone in the desert about thirty miles from Ur; the labour involved in transporting it must have been considerable. The limestone was broken into uneven chunks. The largest were laid by hand, while the rest, together with a mud mortar, were apparently poured into a sort of coffer dam formed by a line of planks parallel with the wall of the tomb shaft. Once the mixture of mud and stone dried, the planks could be removed and the walls built to their full height, then plastered either with mud or occasionally with a fine lime plaster. Woolley compares this method to the techniques used for pouring reinforced concrete. The real surprise was the methods of roofing used in the tombs. Woolley was able to identify both barrel and corbel vaulting, as well as the true dome, set on pendentives. These transformed the square ground plan of the tomb chamber into a circle, over which the dome could be erected. There were also examples of tombs with apsidal ends, covered with half-domes. Sometimes evidence for the centring used in building the domes and vaults could still be seen as holes in the walls. In addition to these remarkable finds, the doorways leading into the tombs were sometimes covered with the true arch, although flat lintels of wood were also present. The technical mastery displayed in the mid-third millennium by these finds upset all the conventional ideas on architectural developments.

Many questions remain to be answered about these graves; for example, as mentioned above, it is not clear if there was any sort of memorial or chapel raised above them, although elaborate rituals were plainly carried out as the shafts were filled in. The presence of human sacrifices has also puzzled archaeologists and historians, as there are no documentary references to such practices. Such written evidence as there is points to a gloomy view of the Sumerian afterlife in the third millennium. In the *Epic of Gilgamesh* it is described as a grey and dismal place with disconsolate ghosts wandering through it. This has led scholars to suggest that if you aspired to a decent quality of life after death, you needed to take with you all the things necessary to achieve it, with a surplus to give as presents to the gods of the Underworld. If you could not afford this yourself, your best hope was either to have a great many sons who would look after your needs following your death, or to attach yourself to the train of a rich and important person. This, Woolley suggested, was the explanation for the attendant bodies in the royal tombs. He painted a dignified scene of the victims filing into the great death pits outside the main tomb chamber to the sound of music provided by the harps and lyres he discovered. Carts drawn by oxen brought in further goods. Each person carried a small cup filled with poison, and, having composed themselves, drank it down. Later, other people arranged the ranks of the dead, killed the animals and filled in the tomb shaft, making further offerings and, occasionally, further burials as they did so.

Recently, some scepticism has been expressed about this solemn scene. It has become possible to look again at some of the few surviving skeletal remains, and a number of surprising facts have emerged. Some of the bones seem to have been 'heat-treated' or partially burnt before burial, and then treated with a compound of mercury, perhaps in order to preserve them. This could mean that the people in the death pits may not have all died at the same time, and some may already have been dead before being put in the grave. Two skulls, one of a 'lady in waiting' and the other of a soldier, provided evidence of blunt trauma – presumably the cause of death. The soldier had been dressed after death; his helmet had been put on back to front. We are beginning to see a rather different picture, which raises two important questions: how willingly did these people go to their deaths? And were they in fact what they appeared to be? Although the number of skulls examined is tiny, it is beginning to look as if some, at least, of the attendants were dead when put into the tomb. It also raises the further possibility that they may not have been the court ladies and guards they appear to be. It has been suggested that they were prisoners of war, who were seen as on a level with animals, and thus suitable as sacrifices. A new programme of research studying the ratios of various strontium isotopes found in the skulls may tell us whether the people killed in the graves were local or not. It has also been suggested that the ritual of the burials was a device used by the early rulers to consolidate the power of their dynasty by what has been called the 'theatre of cruelty'. Certainly, human sacrifice was only practised for a short time by the earliest-known rulers of the city.

The mystery of who the people were who were buried with such pomp still remains unsolved. If we look at them in the wider context of the whole cemetery, it becomes clear that the number of graves in it are not sufficient to account for all the inhabitants of the city of Ur over a period of perhaps three or four hundred years. It is also clear that some sections of society are not represented. For example, there are very few children in the cemetery in spite of the inevitably high infant death rate. This, in turn, suggests that some special qualification was required for interment in this particular cemetery, and Susan Pollock (see further reading) has suggested that the people all belonged to one of the great households of the time – that is to say, to either the court or the household of the high priest or priestess. Such a suggestion is very plausible. It would explain the inclusion of workers with their tools, who are found in the private graves, as well as the wealthy individuals. Nor does this suggestion rule out Woolley's conviction that they were genuinely royal burials, in spite of the problems raised by their omission from the King List.

There is at least one possible explanation for this omission. The answer could be that the people buried in the Ur graves were not actually kings and queens, but were, for example, high-ranking priests and priestesses. This was a popular theory for a time and was elaborated further to suggest that not only were they priests or priestesses, but also participants in the annual ceremony of the sacred marriage, carried out to ensure the future fertility of the land, who were then killed after the ceremony. Woolley destroyed this theory by pointing out that if this were the case, one would expect more graves and an equal number of men's and women's graves. It would also be reasonable to expect the women to be young and nubile, although, as far as Puabi was concerned, this was certainly not the case. In addition, there is only one case where a male and a female tomb are found close together: RG800, the tomb of Puabi, is closely associated with RG789, the grave of what is presumed from the grave goods to be that of a male. Woolley suggested, based on intuition rather than hard fact, that this supposed male had been the husband. In fact, a new analysis of these graves suggests that there may well have been a third tomb chamber as yet undiscovered. This theory rests on the fact that, uniquely, Puabi's tomb lies below the level of 'her' death pit and, in fact, may not belong to it at all. Thus, her death pit, and a putative third tomb chamber, may remain to be found.

If these are priestly graves, there is a further problem. How do we explain the royal titles on some of the grave goods? Perhaps they were funerary gifts from the ruling dynasty, but even if this is the case and the graves are those of priests, it does not solve the fundamental problem presented by the King List. The inscriptions still give us hard archaeological evidence for a dynasty not recorded in it. In the end it seems that, in spite of this problem, Woolley's interpretation of the graves as royal answers most of the questions most convincingly. Scholars will, no doubt, continue to speculate, stimulated by new information coming to light as the result of new analyses.

The bulk of the graves in the cemetery are different and appear to belong to people from every sector of society, from the very poor, buried with nothing but a clay saucer, to the rich, dressed in similar finery to that found in the royal graves. The number of graves is not great enough to account for all the inhabitants of Ur over a period of several centuries, so they probably represent a subsection of the population, defined by the fact that they served in the households of those in the royal graves. As already noted, few graves contain children, but one such is very rich, PG1068, and thus nicknamed the grave of the little princess. Other unusual graves include PG1312, where the male burial is accompanied by female jewellery, as was the case with the grave of Meskalamdug, and a female burial, PG1130, with jewellery rather like Puabi's second 'diadem'. This was a charming choker necklace of lapis lazuli and gold, decorated with little figures of flowers and animals in gold. In spite of these luxurious objects, PG755 discussed earlier, the grave of Meskalamdug, is still the richest of them all. The majority of the private graves are inhumations at the bottom of a shaft. Some bodies were buried wrapped in matting, some in wooden or clay coffins, but all seem to have had a mat laid over them and grave goods provided before the shaft was filled in. There is no standard orientation to the graves or to the bodies, but the body always lies on its side with the knees slightly bent, and the hands usually in front of the face. In many of the graves, there are a large number of plain saucers of clay, and by analogy with other sites we can suggest that these may have been used for funerary libations, then thrown into the grave.

Two groups of graves of approximately the same age can be isolated because of their contents. The first consists of poorly furnished male graves found in Pit W on the edge of the cemetery: each has a dagger or other weapon, and most have a large shell cylinder seal. Where the design is legible, it is always of a contest scene and this, coupled with the ubiquitous daggers, led Woolley to suggest that this was the military sector of the cemetery. One of these graves was unique and held the only stone statue found in the cemetery. The statue shows a charming small woman standing with her hands clasped in front of her. She wears a fillet in her hair and the traditional sheepskin garment, with one shoulder bare. She looks like the dedicatory statues found in temples across the Sumerian world, where they were apparently thought to intercede with the deity on behalf of the person portrayed. Perhaps the soldier hoped she would intercede for him in the Underworld?

Another distinctive group is formed by Woolley's burnt graves. There are not very many of them: seventeen can be assigned to the group, with another eleven possible examples. They are not all the same date: the majority are dug into the grey level which sealed the royal graves, and so belong to the later EDIIIb phase. At least one was found below this, and so may belong to EDIIIa. One is dated to the Sargonid period.

The bodies are also buried in a variety of different ways: some in wicker coffins, some in clay ones, and some wrapped in matting. They all show evidence of partial burning, apparently in situ, of the head and upper body – something found nowhere else in the cemetery. The grave goods do not mark them out as unusual, and, as a rule, the graves are not particularly well furnished. There is one exception to this: PG156. This is quite a rich grave. The partial burning marks these burials out as a distinctive group with beliefs and rituals not found elsewhere, but whether they were united by profession or by origins or by some other tie, we shall never know.

As in earlier periods, there is relatively little evidence for structures from the Early Dynastic period within the sacred enclosure. There are probably two main reasons for this: the first is the massive erosion that which has taken place across the site and the evidence for which can be seen in the stratigraphy of Pit F, for example. The second is the habit of enclosing older religious buildings inside or below later models because they were too holy to destroy. The remains of an impressive terrace wall were found around the *temenos*, with a stone footing of blocks of unworked limestone four feet high. Above this rose a mud-brick superstructure decorated with shallow buttresses. Just enough plano-convex brick was recovered by Woolley to suggest that an earlier, smaller ziggurat or high terrace existed inside that of Ur-Nammu and that the older ziggurat terrace had housed important buildings, probably including a temple whose plans it was impossible to piece together. Two other structures were identified on the terrace, the first as the temple where the food of the gods was cooked in the northern corner, and the other in the eastern corner, as a shrine to the moon god's wife Ningal and several subsidiary deities. Some evidence for inlay was recovered from the courtyard of the second, which shows the use of composite figures at about one-third life size with steatite wigs and shell faces in the decoration. Such evidence as there is suggests the scenes were even more elaborate than those recovered at contemporary al Ubaid. In one of the guard-rooms on either side of the entrance gate, Woolley found a large quantity of clay sling bullets and balls. He interpreted these as belonging to the temple armoury, for use in case of attack, because, as we have seen, there was constant jockeying for position among the city states of the Mesopotamian plain.

Some scrappy evidence for housing was found at the so-called EH site, which lies outside the Third Dynasty temenos wall to the south. This area was originally dug by J. E. Taylor in the 1880s, but he found no coherent plans, as it was badly disturbed by drains of the early second millennium. Woolley was able to confirm the presence of plano-convex brick walls over the whole area, but even he could not piece together much evidence for the housing they represented. He did establish that the third-millennium houses, like the early second-millennium ones, had elaborate drains, made up of pottery rings or pots with holes in them superimposed to form drains up to thirty or forty feet deep. These drains were packed round with sherds of pottery and were in use for generations.

Art and Technology: Objects from the Royal Cemetery

Having looked at the building of the royal graves and discussed who may have been buried in them, it is time to look at some of the objects found in them and in the other graves in the cemetery to see what they tell us about Ur in the middle of the third millennium BC. Woolley's finds revolutionized the perception of the artistic and technological achievements of third-millennium Mesopotamia. They also placed the city of Ur at the centre of a far flung trade and exchange network stretching into Central Asia and the Indus valley. Ur was not unique in its acquisition of foreign goods, as similar luxuries are found at other sites in south Mesopotamia, although never in such abundance. (This may be the result of the accident of recovery, for no other 'royal' graves have been excavated either.) What was exchanged for these foreign luxuries is less easy to explain, as few goods of Mesopotamian origin have been found outside the region. Almost by default, we have to assume that many of the exports were of perishable materials, like textiles for instance, and so leave little trace in the archaeological record.

By the end of the third millennium, there are large numbers of cuneiform texts from which it is possible to describe the workings of a textile industry, part of which was in the hands of the palace. There are no such archives for the Early Dynastic period. It does not seem to be stretching the evidence too far to suggest that something similar, but probably much smaller, may have existed in the mid-third millennium too. It is difficult to see what goods other than textiles could have been used in exchange for all the exotic foreign items found at Ur.

The archaeological evidence is also unhelpful in the search for Mesopotamia's exports, and it has not been possible to identify any 'factories' in the scrappy remains of buildings of this period uncovered at Ur. However, the importance of Ur as a political and economic force on the Sumerian plain is beyond doubt.

It seems that it was not unique, but was one of a number of small, independent city states that from time to time were brought together under the rule of a single exceptional ruler, only to fall apart into their old rivalries on his death. The first time we can show this happening is later in the third millennium, when a king of Uruk called Lugalzagesi overthrew Ur and briefly united the southern plain under his rule.

There is such a range of objects in such a variety of materials in the cemetery that it is difficult to know how to present them. There are precious and non-precious metals worked in a number of different ways and used for many purposes; there are semi-precious stones for beads and more utilitarian ones used for making containers; there are shells from as far away as India; there is pottery, and in rare cases the traces of organic materials such as wood survive. There is jewellery: headdresses, earrings, amulets, beads, pins, seals and more exotic objects like the cloak of Puabi (the female main burial from RG800) that is made up of strings of beads. There are weapons and armour, some designed purely for display and some for lethal purposes. There are vehicles and model boats. There are the remains of furniture. There are musical instruments. There are containers of many different sorts, some still containing traces of

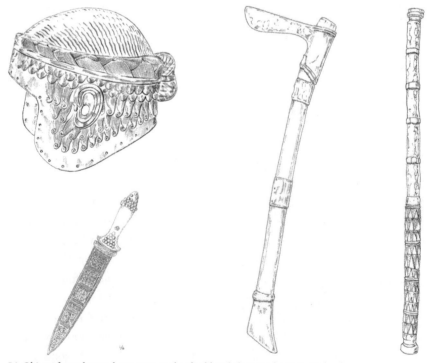

5.i Objects from the royal cemetery made of gold and electrum by Tessa Rickards

the food originally contained in them (Fig. 5.i). This was apparently to provide nourishment in the poorly resourced Underworld. Most of the objects were excavated personally by Woolley and his wife Katharine, and they were meticulously recorded. Sometimes, Woolley was involved not only in 'first aid' in the field to enable him to lift and pack the objects, but also with the cleaning and reconstruction undertaken in the British Museum when the objects allocated to the museum had been transported to Britain at the end of each season. What follows is a description of a selection of these objects to try to demonstrate, on the one hand, the richness of Woolley's finds and the skill with which they were uncovered, and, on the other, the wealth of the city of Ur (Fig. 5.ii).

One of the most spectacular finds in the cemetery was the elaborate headdress worn by Puabi. It was made up of many different elements and was restored by Katharine Woolley. The wreaths formed the major part of it and were of such large dimensions that it seems the lady must have been wearing a wig in order to support all its elements. Round this wig, gold ribbons were draped criss-cross, visible largely from behind. Above the ribbons were wreaths of two different sorts of gold leaves, and another of gold rings. Above these was a rope of lapis and carnelian beads interspersed with eight-leaved rosettes. The whole creation was topped by a magnificent comb or mantilla of gold, ending in seven gold spikes, each decorated with a gold rosette. The lady also wore a gold necklace, ten finger rings, gold spiral hair ornaments and enormous boat-shaped gold

5.ii Jewellery from the royal cemetery made of gold and electrum by Tessa Rickards

earrings. The attendant women wore scaled-down versions of this headdress, sometimes with silver ribbons, for example, or fewer wreaths, while the combs were decorated with fewer rosettes.

From her neck to her waist, Puabi wore a large number of beads in strings. Woolley restored these as an elaborate cape, originally with a fabric backing for the beads, while he saw the beads round her leg as a garter. Another piece of jewellery lay by her head, on what Woolley thought might have been a small wooden table. Woolley restored it as a diadem, but this reconstruction has been questioned and it may in fact be composed of the parts of six smaller pieces. It is made up of rows of small lapis beads parallel to one another and trimmed with gold beads along the edges. It has various small amulets suspended from it, including pairs of recumbent sheep, deer, stags and bearded bulls. These are interspersed with small, gold, plant-like objects with fruit and flowers of carnelian and lapis on them. Finally, there are some elaborately twisted pendants of gold wire. It is a delightful object. Puabi also owned a gold 'toilet set'. These are found quite frequently and are usually composed of a group of up to three or four small tools. Woolley identified these as tweezers (for eyebrow plucking?), a pointed tool (for cleaning nails etc.?) and a tool with a rounded end (for applying eye paint?). There were also a few tiny chisel-like tools. They are often found together in a little sheath of metal, which can be covered in leather. These sets occur in various metals throughout the cemetery, and are complemented by shells filled with kohl and other cosmetic paints.

The pieces of jewellery illustrate well the international links of the rulers of Ur. All the materials from which they are made had to be imported. Lapis lazuli was extremely popular and was probably thought to have magical powers; it can only have come from Badakshan, to the east of Afghanistan. We still do not know where the other materials originated. The gold and silver may have come from Anatolia, the carnelian from the Deccan or perhaps from eastern Arabia, while the agate probably originated on the Iranian plateau. In most cases, these precious stones were probably imported in semi-worked form and finished locally to suit local tastes. There is at least one exception to this: a group of carnelian beads with white geometric patterns etched on to them, made in the Indus valley. The process of manufacture is elaborate and there is no evidence for such a technique being known outside the Indus region.

The women did not have a monopoly on 'bling', though the men were not as lavishly decorated. The typical male headdress is referred to as a *br'm*, something rather akin to the ropes used today by men in the Arab world for keeping their head cloths in place. The ancient ones were made of plaited metal chains with three large beads of lapis, gold or carnelian over the forehead. The women might also wear necklaces and earrings, and carry weapons, which, in the case of main male burials, could be of precious metals decorated in many ways. The most striking example of this is the helmet of Meskalamdug (PG755), who, it has been suggested, might have been the crown prince. This item is made in a perfect simulacrum of the elaborate hairstyle worn by the kings of the day, complete with chignon at the back, tied with a fillet, and small kiss curls hanging down. There are holes all around the edges of the helmet, presumably to allow the attachment of a lining. This suggests it was probably meant to be worn on ceremonial occasions, as the electrum of which it is made would have offered little protection in battle. Another superb object is a dagger found in RG580, a badly disturbed royal tomb: it has a gold blade and a lapis handle decorated with small gold studs. The sheath is also of gold, decorated with an elaborate basketwork pattern and more gold studs. Whetstones of lapis and other materials are often found with the daggers, presumably to keep them in good working order. Although weapons are usually found with men, the main female body in RG1054 has both a dagger and a whetstone.

There are also gold, electrum and silver axes and spears, sometimes occurring in bundles or sets, and many more copper* daggers. Some of these weapons are marked with a symbol apparently representing a bull's leg, and it may be that such weapons were issued by some central authority to the soldiers in its army. On the other hand, it could be a maker's mark. The axes could be socketed or tanged, though the latter tend to be later in date, and the blades are either at right angles to the shaft or transverse to it. One electrum example from PG755, the grave of Meskalamdug, is an unusual double crescentic axe with a blade on either side of the shaft. One or two other types are not matched elsewhere in Mesopotamia and may have been of foreign origin. The soldier guards in the graves wear simple copper helmets without decoration and may have worn leather cloaks with round copper plaques on them, like those illustrated on the so-called Standard of Ur (p. 65). There is no evidence for other types of protection for the soldiers except for the remains of what may have been a shield from RG789, the so-called king's grave, with a fine design of striding lions, but it is so fragmentary that it is difficult to be sure what it was.

Plenty of other metal artefacts do not fit tidily into the categories of jewellery or weapons. A number of spatulate objects, usually of copper, Woolley called

---

* The term 'copper' is used loosely for both the pure metal and the alloys, notably those of copper and arsenic or occasionally copper and tin.

razors, though they look blunt, and there are tools like chisels and saws, including some examples in precious metals. Puabi, who really does seem to have had everything, has examples in gold in her grave. Are they perhaps symbolic of the ruler's duty to build and maintain the temples of the city god? If this suggestion is allowed, then can we perhaps see the dagger and whetstone found with the female main burial in RG1054 as symbolic of the ruler's duty to protect his/her people? Both precious and non-precious metals are used for a wide variety of containers, including some beautiful fluted goblets in gold and silver as well as a variety of bowls, some with handles – apparently for suspension – and some without. There are also vessels that seem to be precious-metal copies of conch shells (which are found in the Gulf of Oman and the Indian Ocean). The shells themselves were found in a number of graves, cut down, often decorated, and probably used for pouring libations, as were the metal copies.

Containers of stone are also common and include a spouted bowl carved out of a single piece of lapis lazuli and another of obsidian, both spectacular technical achievements given the nature of the stones, as well as jars and bowls of a translucent calcite whose natural veining provides decorative patterning on the exterior of the vessel. One little 'box' of the same material, subdivided into four compartments, would originally have had a lid, and probably held cosmetics. Unfortunately, the lid was not found. The nearest parallels for such a box are from an area stretching from north-east Iran into Central Asia. The lapis we know must have come from far to the north-east in Badakshan and the calcite is probably from eastern Iran. One or two pots are made of a stone, variously described as chlorite or steatite, which is relatively soft and easy to decorate. In other parts of contemporaneous south Mesopotamia, pots of this stone, magnificently decorated with human, animal and monstrous figures, are sometimes inlaid with coloured stones. At Ur, the examples found only have geometric patterns, but are of the same stone and belong to the same tradition. Recently, a manufacturing area for such items has been found in south-western Iran, so here is another indication of Ur's widespread contacts. Some of the most unusual containers from the cemetery are made of ostrich eggshells cut open and decorated round the rim and foot with inlay. Sometimes they have necks and feet of clay attached and these were then decorated. There is one luxury model made of gold from RG779, where a number of silver examples were also found, but could not be repaired. The original eggs may have come from the Arabian Peninsula, or from the Syrian desert.

The only stone object that does not fit into these categories is the small standing figure of a woman referred to in the previous chapter, which was found

5.iii Female statue from a soldier's grave by Mary Shepperson

in the proposed military cemetery. She is made of what is probably local white limestone, with lapis and shell eyes and an inlaid fillet round her face (Fig. 5.iii). The eyebrows were originally inlaid too, but the inlay has fallen out. She is in the tradition of votive statues, wearing fleecy garments and with clasped hands, found widely in shrines of the EDIII period, where they are thought to have interceded endlessly on behalf of the donor.

Sea and river shell, including mother-of-pearl, is widely found and most commonly used as inlay, either cut to shape as part of a composite figure or engraved with designs that included humans and animals. Three spectacular objects decorated in this way stand out: the so-called Standard of Ur and the two animals known as the 'rams in the thicket'. In addition, there were gaming boards, boxes, chests, musical instruments and other objects decorated in the same way. The 'Standard' is from RG779, and was almost certainly not a standard, but may originally have been the body of a musical instrument. In its reconstructed state, it is made up of two panels of mosaic back to back, each measuring 47 centimetres by 20 centimetres, and is bordered with mosaic. The design is divided into three registers. Each side has a different theme, one side showing a battle and its aftermath with prisoners being paraded before the victor, while the other shows provisions being brought in for the banquet presumably given to celebrate the victory. Each register seems to have been 'read' from left to right and to culminate in the figure shown in the centre of the top one. The weapons and clothing of the soldiers shown appear to be very similar to those found with the actual soldiers in the royal graves, while the four-wheeled carts depicted – the equivalent of a modern tank – are probably similar to those in the burial pits. Each vehicle contains two soldiers, one to drive and a second to fight. One is seen in the act of throwing a spear. The rein rings, which are shown on the reins of the equids drawing the carts, are identical to actual examples from the tombs, including a famous likeness of an onager, made of electrum.

The rams in the thickets are magnificent pieces of skilled artisanship, but, like the Standard, their function is unclear. It has been suggested that they too may have decorated musical instruments, which, as we shall see, frequently have an animal head on the front. The rams may have been conceived of as a pair, but one is slightly taller than the other. They come from a corner of the Great Death Pit RG1237: the one now in Philadelphia stands 42.6 centimetres tall. Each animal stands on its hind legs with its front hooves resting on the golden branches of a plant. These branches end in large gold rosettes. The body of the animal was made on a wooden frame originally covered with silver, now in a poor state, while its fleece is depicted by pieces of shell individually cut and attached to the body with bitumen, as were the lapis elements of the fleece on the neck and shoulders, the lapis horns, beard, pupils and eyebrows. The animal at the British Museum is arrogantly male, and both have a gold cylinder protruding vertically from the back of the neck. This must have supported either a small table, as Woolley originally suggested, or perhaps the frame of a musical instrument.

Several musical instruments were recovered from the royal graves and are divided by Woolley into lyres (the more common) and harps. The recovery of the so-called plaster lyre from PG1151 is a splendid example of Woolley's skill as an excavator. The first sign of an unusual find came when a worker found a row of holes going down into the soil, two square and the rest round. Intrigued, Woolley poured liquid plaster of Paris down the holes and left it to dry. Then the earth was peeled away to reveal the shape of a lyre with the inlaid decoration of the sounding box still in place, and the head of a bull or cow in copper on the front of it. The square holes belonged to the frame of the instrument and the round holes to the strings. He went on to find several more lyres and at least two harps, all beautifully decorated with mosaic or engraved shell plaques and with animal heads on the front. The most splendid example of these heads is made of gold and lapis, with a beautifully curled lapis beard attached to its muzzle, from RG789, the king's grave. Below the head on the front of the sounding box was an engraved plaque with three inlaid registers. These depict a hero struggling with two human-headed bulls in the top one, and, below this, animals on their hind legs serving a meal, while an animal plays a harp like the one the plaque adorns. In addition to the stringed instruments, the badly decayed remains of silver tubes with holes in them in PG333 are probably the remains of double pipes. Music seems to have played an important role in entertainment and ritual and we can see two musicians entertaining the guests on the banquet side of the Standard: one holds a harp and the second may be a singer.

A number of other very fine animal heads representing lions, bulls and stags were also found, in gold, silver and copper. Some, like the small lions' heads from RG800, probably decorated furniture, perhaps as the finials of armrests on throne-like chairs. Other heads from the same grave may have decorated the chariot. The vehicle appears to have had runners rather than wheels, enabling it to run smoothly on sand. The carts probably brought the heavier goods into the death pits and had solid wooden wheels. One of the easiest and most comfortable methods of transport must have been by boat up and down the waterways and a number of long, elegant model boats were found, some of silver and some of bitumen. They were propelled by long oars or, in one case, by a type of punt pole. Similar boats were to be seen in the Marshes of Iraq until the time of Saddam Hussein, when the draining of the marshes drove the people out. As parts of the marshes are now being repopulated, the boats are beginning to return.

The most numerous finds from the cemetery area, as in most digs, were pieces of pottery. This was usually undecorated and rather utilitarian, perhaps because there were so many metal and stone jugs, bowls and pots of all descriptions for display purposes. There are a few exceptions: for example, bottle-shaped, carefully ridged brown pots are found in a number of royal graves. These originated on the upper Euphrates in Syria. They must have contained some special imported materials, such as scented oils perhaps, in order to qualify for inclusion in these richly furnished tombs. It is also curious that one type of pot widely found at other contemporaneous sites hardly appears at all at Ur. This jar, with an upright handle, is decorated with crude depictions of a female face and sometimes body. There is only one example recorded from Ur (U.10103), but elsewhere they are one of the type of fossils of the period and are frequently associated with a high-stemmed shallow bowl, often referred to as an offering stand, which does occur at Ur. The pottery was all wheel-made and most appears to be local, so somewhere outside the temenos area it is reasonable to suggest that there must be a potters' quarter.

An important group of finds, not yet described, is made up of the many cylinder seals found throughout the third-millennium levels and especially in the cemetery. They could almost be called the signature find of the third millennium, as they occur in increasing numbers throughout the period and had many uses. They were used as signatures, as authorizations, as amulets, and perhaps as trade marks as well. Each design was intended to be unique, although the range of subject matter was restricted, and sometimes inscriptions were added, stating the name and position of the owner. These cuneiform inscriptions had to be engraved in mirror writing so that as the seal was rolled on the damp clay the writing appeared correctly. The subject matter and the style of the seals changed over time, and these changes have often been used by archaeologists as a relative-dating tool, both for the seal itself and for its context. This is not an entirely satisfactory procedure, as it does not take account of good and bad craftspeople, or of different places developing their own stylistic variants: both factors may disrupt the carefully organized sequence. There is also the problem of heirlooms. People might use a seal that had been in the family for several generations before it finally went out of use. Used with these problems in mind, seals still provide us with an extremely useful chronological tool, especially when used in conjunction with other evidence. The designs on them also provide a window into the concerns and beliefs of the people who wore them.

The most popular designs on the seals from the royal cemetery are probably the combat seals. These have depictions of stylized fights between pairs of animals standing on their hind legs, or hero figures and animals, with a few monsters to boot, notably the human-headed bull. There are also banquet scenes similar to that on the Standard described earlier, showing both men and women eating and drinking. Two, or even three, registers can be found on some seals, with elaborate scenes on each. The materials used for seals vary from gold and silver to shell (the latter is so badly preserved that the design may be illegible) and the quality of the work varies greatly. Attempts have been made to match certain designs to certain relevant professions, but although some correlation was observed between the graves of soldiers and shell seals with combat scenes, the match was far from perfect, and many other high-status seals, both male and female, show the same type of design. Some of the seals show enormous verve and a great sense of movement, even though the depiction of people is schematic. It is curious that the artists of the day seem to have been far better at portraying animals than people on their seals; the same is also true of the people and animals shown on the shell plaques. The position of some seals found in the graves and some depictions on inlays, most notably from Mari, show that the seal was worn suspended on a string with two or three large beads, from the opening in the head of the pins, which were used to hold garments together. Some of the largest specimens of seals, mainly from earlier periods, may have been kept in an office for use on formal business documents, as they are rather large to be worn.

This chapter has provided a very superficial view of some of the artefacts from the royal cemetery. Many are beautiful, some are useful, and some combine these attributes. Two aspects of the finds, especially the metal finds, have not yet been discussed: first, the origin of the raw materials and second, the techniques used to produce the objects.

The far-flung origins of some of the stones used have already been noted. The metals present are gold, electrum, silver, lead, tin bronze, and most common of all, copper, sometimes with an admixture of arsenic or antimony. Traces of nickel also occur. Gold and silver seem to have been quite freely available, the silver probably coming from the metal-rich areas of central Anatolia around Ergani Maden, which may also have provided some of the copper. The origin of the gold is a mystery, but it is probably alluvial and may also have come from Anatolia, although further to the north and west. Several of the 'gold' artefacts, such as Meskalamdug's helmet, were shown by analysis to be made of electrum, a mixture of gold and silver. This can occur in nature, but was more likely to have been deliberately alloyed by the goldsmiths to produce metals of contrasting colours. There is, for example, a silver bowl decorated with contrasting strips of electrum.[†] Lead was not widely used at this period, and is closely allied to silver. It, too, probably came from Anatolia. Some copper, as we have seen, may have come from around Ergani Maden, but other sources are also probable and deposits in north-west Iran, in the mountains of Oman, and even as far away as the Indus valley seem likely. The source of the tin, which was used sparingly to make bronze, is still hotly debated, but polymetallic areas have now been identified in western Afghanistan and in western Iran. Both these are perfectly feasible as source areas.

The metals were probably imported into Ur as ingots or in semi-finished form, as it would not have been cost-effective to transport large amounts of unprocessed ore, much of which would then be discarded as slag after smelting.

---

† The bowl was found in RG800, excavation number U10891, and is said to be in Baghdad.

There is also a problem in southern Iraq with a lack of good fuel, which would have made smelting difficult, though burnt date stones are said to make excellent charcoal. Once the metals had been acquired, the craftspeople seem to have had a great range of techniques at their disposal. Sheet gold, silver and copper were used to coat objects modelled in bitumen or wood. Some of the magnificent animal heads are modelled on a bitumen or wood base, while others were cast. In both cases, the details were then engraved to finish the piece. The little gold amulets of animals on Puabi's 'diadem' were made this way. Casting was widely practised both in open and closed moulds, while the lost-wax process was also known. Objects such as the great boat-shaped gold earrings worn by Puabi and her attendants were made in two halves and then sweated or soldered together. Decorative techniques included cloisonné work, filigree, and the elaborate plaiting and twisting of strips of gold to form chains. It used to be thought that the jewellers had also mastered the art of granulation, but recently some of the objects were re-examined, and on all but one example the granulation turned out to be tiny gold nails rather than true granulation.

The sophisticated technology and skill shown not only by the metalwork, but also by the stonework and the seals, allows us to make more deductions about the city of Ur in the middle of the third millennium BC. The high levels of skill involved strongly suggest the presence of full-time specialist craftsmen, in addition to the merchants who provided the raw materials. There must also have been a rigorous training programme for these craftspeople and it is likely that this was provided by apprenticeships, usually kept within a family group, so that fathers trained sons and nephews, and occasionally daughters, to take over the business. It is not clear if all these craftsmen worked for one of the great institutions, the temple or the state, or whether they worked for themselves. It seems likely that some were 'tied' to the temple or palace and were rewarded with goods for their subsistence, and sometimes with grants of agricultural land. They may also have worked freelance some of the time, while others may have worked entirely in the private sector. Much still remains to be learnt about the workings of the economy at this period, but, as the bulk of the surviving administrative material comes from temple archives, our picture is rather distorted. There is hardly any information about what might be called the private sector.

It is, however, clear that Ur was hugely prosperous at this time, and was home to a vast array of people with different skills. It is not possible to estimate the population figures because so little of the city has been excavated outside the sacred area, and it is clear that much of the Early Dynastic town has been destroyed by erosion and by the constant rebuilding through the centuries.

Evidence like that from the burnt graves in the cemetery, where a different burial rite seems to have been used, suggests the possibility that not all the inhabitants were native-born. It is entirely possible that merchants from foreign lands, engaged in these long-distance trading ventures from places such as the Indus valley and central Anatolia, were resident in the city for at least some of the time. This possibility is made more likely by the finds of a small number of seals in the style of the Harappan civilization, but, sadly, none of them is well stratified, so their dating is problematic.

Combining the evidence discussed in this and the previous chapter demonstrates that Ur was a major centre at this time, and it is probably fair to describe it as the heart of a city state. This state was ruled by people, whether priests or kings, who were immensely wealthy and who had the power of life and death over the city's inhabitants. These included large numbers of skilled craftspeople and other professionals, such as the scribes who served as a civil service. The town may have been organized into areas by crafts and by skills. It has already been suggested that these usually ran in families. The heads of the families in each 'quarter' probably had some degree of responsibility for law and order within it, while the young men may have been liable for military service or corveé (mandatory) labour. The majority of the inhabitants were agricultural labourers who travelled out of town every day to produce some of the city's food requirements, while workmen and women carried out the tasks necessary to produce goods for export, or to build major public works such as temples. We can also suggest that there was probably a formal system of laws and the presence of a body to enforce it.

Ur was not unique. It stood on equal terms with a number of other city states on the southern plain of Iraq. Each seems to have been politically independent, but they were united by a common cultural tradition.

The Defeat of the City State of Ur by the Rulers of Akkad

By the middle of the third millennium BC, the southern plains were home to a number of rather fractious city states, including Ur. Although politically independent, they were closely linked by their shared material culture and their proximity. Today the rulers of these states are often described as kings, but there are a number of titles in Sumerian, such as *ensi* and *lugal*, whose exact significance we do not know. One title, in particular, stands out and seems to have had special importance. The title King of Kish, a city lying to the north-east of Ur, seems to have been held by rulers who briefly managed to subdue one or more of their neighbours and seems to imply some sort of wider suzerainty. One of the kings of the royal cemetery, Meskalamdug, held this title in addition to his title of King of Ur, but after his death Ur seems to have declined in political significance and his immediate successors no longer claimed the wider title.

As we have seen, it is generally thought on the basis of the stratigraphy at Ur (see Chapter 4) that the dynasty of Mesannepadda succeeded that of the royal graves and Meskalamdug. Both the dynasty of the royal graves and that of Mesannepadda were contemporaneous with the ruling dynasty at the city of Lagash, another of the city states of the southern plain. The art produced in the reign of its second ruler, Ur-Nanše, and his two successors has very close parallels with that from the royal cemetery period. This Lagash Dynasty, like the Kalamdug Dynasty, is excluded from the King List, but it has been possible to reconstruct it from the inscriptions of the rulers themselves. The third ruler of the Lagash Dynasty, Eannatum, was a successful warrior who defeated Lagash's neighbour, Umma, with which there had been a long-running feud over a stretch of disputed territory.

This is the victory commemorated in text and pictures on the famous Stela of the Vultures. This narrates the whole history of the dispute in words and depicts the final god-given victory in pictures. The stela also provides us with a picture of how the weapons found in the royal cemetery were actually used. The relief is made of limestone and is about 180 centimetres (70.9 inches) tall and 139 centimetres (51.2 inches) wide. Each side is divided into registers: four on one side and two on the other. It was probably erected in a public place such as a temple courtyard, so everyone would be made aware of the power of Eannatum, and of the fact he was a favourite of the god Ningirsu, the battle god and patron of Lagash. Ningirsu himself is seen on the top register of the side with only two of them, and is shown as much larger than anyone else portrayed, in order to underline his status. This is a convention seen, too, on the so-called Standard of Ur. Ningirsu holds his dreaded battle net in his left hand and the heads of the defeated men poke out through the mesh. He hits one of these protruding heads with a mace, held in his right hand.

Unfortunately, the rest of the stela is incomplete, but it seems as if Ningirsu is followed by another deity and a standard carrying the image of the lion-headed eagle (his symbol). The eagle is holding the god's battle net together with its talons. The lower register is badly damaged and only the rein ring of a battle chariot can be seen, decorated with a lion and preceded by the crowned head of another deity.

On the other face of the stela, the human narrative can be seen, and the story was probably meant to be read from top to bottom. The top register shows Eannatum leading his heavily armed infantry into battle. Their arms and those of the king can be exactly matched in the royal cemetery at Ur. The king's helmet is a faithful representation of the gold helmet found in the grave of Meskalamdug. In front of the king is a heap of dead enemy soldiers whose heads are being carried off by vultures. The second register is more fragmentary, but shows the king in his chariot armed with a long spear and leading a group of soldiers, who also carry long spears. The third fragment seems to show the aftermath of the battle, with a neatly laid out pile of corpses being covered with earth, while offerings are being made by a large figure of which only one foot and a bit of skirt survives. Presumably, this is Eannatum himself. Perhaps it is his own dead being buried here, while the enemy bodies seen in the top register are left to the mercy of scavengers. The bottom register is the worst-preserved of all and only a long spear pointing directly at the eye of a human head can be seen. Eannatum not only subdued Umma, but went on to claim victory over a number of other city states including Ur and Uruk, another of Ur's neighbours.

Eannatum's second successor, Enmetena (Entemena), was also a warrior and has left a number of monuments detailing his conquests. One of his less-bellicose monuments, a now headless statue, was found at Ur and seems had been erected at a gate to the temple precinct in the seventh century BC, when it was already an antique. It had probably originally stood in the temple of the moon god. It is interesting that this statue is made of diorite, a hard shiny black stone possibly from Iran or Arabia. It became a favourite for royal statues in the succeeding Agade Dynasty. The statue has an inscription on its shoulder detailing what may be a land grant to a temple, but does not specifically mention Ur. The statue was looted from the Iraq Museum after the invasion in 2003 but, fortunately, was eventually retrieved by the Americans from a warehouse in Brooklyn and returned to Iraq. It seems that Ur had already declined in importance by the time of Enmetena and very little, except their names, is known of the three rulers who apparently succeeded Aannepadda, son of Mesannepadda.

Uruk soon broke away from Lagash and managed to subdue first Ur and then Lagash itself. However, another shake of the political kaleidoscope saw Uruk once more in the ascendancy and Lugalzagesi, its ruler, claiming – perhaps not very convincingly – to have conquered all the lands from the Mediterranean to the head of the Persian Gulf. He called these the Upper and the Lower Sea. This so-called conquest was probably more in the nature of a raid accompanied by some looting and destruction of property; it is doubtful if he had the human resources to subdue such a wide area. What is definitely known, however, is that Lugalzagesi himself was later defeated by a ruler who was to become one of the most iconic figures in the early history of Mesopotamia, Sargon of Agade.

Sargon was apparently a foundling brought up by a gardener who found him by the banks of a canal in a reed basket – a motif repeated in the story of Moses. He became cup-bearer to the King of Kish, a position of considerable importance: he could have observed the business of government at first hand. Before long, he broke away from Kish and established himself with a band of followers in a town called Agade/Akkad. The site of Agade is unknown, but scholars now tend to place it beneath Baghdad itself, or east of the Tigris. The discovery, identification and excavation of Agade would be one of the great prizes of Mesopotamian archaeology. From this base, Sargon rapidly conquered the whole of the southern plain and captured Lugalzagesi of Uruk, though it seems Lugalzagesi was not killed but was allowed to continue as governor of Uruk once he had acknowledged Sargon as his overlord. Like Lugalzagesi before him, Sargon, too, claimed to have washed his weapons in the Upper and Lower Seas, the Mediterranean and the Gulf. He was also able to consolidate his power in an area covering much of what is now north Syria and stretching as far south as Elam in south-western Iran. He passed on his realm to two of his sons, although not without rebellions by the southern cities, and then, eventually, to his famous grandson Naram-Sin.

Naram-Sin was a great warrior who followed in his grandfather's footsteps, re-establishing Agade control over a vast area. He, too, faced a number of rebellions and left behind a striking stela commemorating his victories. This stela broke away from the artistic conventions of the Early Dynastic rulers and of the early Agade period. It had no registers, and the design covered the whole surface. It shows the handsome king with a muscular body striding up a mountain, heavily armed, but clad only in a kilt and a horned helmet, trampling his enemies underfoot. There is also, perhaps for the first time, an attempt to represent the mountain scenery where the victory had taken place. The horned helmet was the traditional mark of a deity, so by wearing it Naram-Sin is portraying himself as divine (Fig. 6.i). This is confirmed by various texts that also refer to him as a god – albeit the god of his city, Akkad, not one of the great gods. Sadly, his power, too, was to prove ephemeral and his reign ended in chaos. His downfall was attributed to his displeasing the gods, not by his hubris in declaring himself divine, but by ignoring omens regarding a building project at Nippur, the religious capital. This was not the end of the dynasty, although the 'empire' shrank with each successive ruler and was eventually reduced to the city of Akkad itself.

The archaeological remains from Ur for the period between the death of Aannepadda and the conquest by Sargon are very sparse, partly because there was a great clearance of the ziggurat and its surroundings, preparatory to a huge building programme by the rulers of the succeeding Third Dynasty of Ur, who

6.i Figure of Naram-Sin from his stela

came to power in about 2150 BC. A number of isolated artefacts date from this time, and have already been described, like the headless statue of Enmetena of Lagash. In addition, a strange square stone plaque with a square hole in the centre is perhaps a little earlier and may be contemporaneous with the royal graves. It is divided into two registers: the top one shows a naked man pouring a libation in front of a seated god. He has a curious sack-like object thrown over one shoulder and behind him are standing three women, the middle one being taller than the others, usually a sign of higher status. All three wear curious hats of a style that later becomes the prerogative of the high priestess of Nannar/Sin, the patron god of Ur. The second register again shows a libation being performed by a nude male, but this time he stands in front of a temple façade. Behind him, facing us, is a female figure like those in the top register, while behind her is a man carrying a kid or a lamb, presumably as an offering. The third figure is another female, in profile, wearing what looks like normal dress. Plaques like this are frequently associated with land transfers or sales, and were attached to temple walls. Perhaps – very speculatively – the couple in the bottom register have made a gift of property to the temple served by the priestesses.

The interest of the Sargonid kings in Ur is demonstrated by a number of inscribed fragments from bowls and other votive objects found carefully buried below the floor of the so-called treasury – the *E-nun-mah* (see Chapter 7) were apparently considered too holy and too precious to be thrown away, even in their broken state. One of the most interesting of the finds from this poorly understood period is an alabaster disc found in the ruins of the *Giparu*, now known as the Enheduanna disc (Fig. 6.iii). This is a roughly circular disc with a scene in relief on one side and an inscription on the other: both were in very poor condition. The inscription mentions the name of Enheduanna, high priestess of Nannar/Sin, who had been appointed by her father, Sargon of Agade. Having a close member of your family as high priest must have been an excellent way of flattering a conquered city and of ensuring that the priesthood, at least, was loyal to you. The temple was also – to judge from the tablets found in the archives from other similar temples – a major economic force, with large tracts of land and 'factories' for the manufacture of textiles, so that it was undoubtedly useful to have these resources, too, under the (indirect) control of the king.

The relief has been heavily and imaginatively restored, and much of the detail is speculative. The scene shows the high priestess, Enheduanna, preceded by a naked man, probably a priest, who pours a libation from a spouted vase, before what has been reconstructed as a ziggurat with four stages. Since it is more usual

6.ii Figure of Enheduanna, high priestess of the moon god

for such libation scenes to take place in front of either a seated deity or a temple façade, and bearing in mind that the ziggurat as it now appears is entirely reconstructed, it should be viewed with some caution. Enheduanna is wearing the traditional fleece dress seen on votive statues from the Early Dynastic period, and the distinctive hat seen on the relief described above. Behind her are one or possibly two, clothed male figures with their hands raised in the traditional gesture of worship and greeting.

As we have seen, there are virtually no architectural remains firmly attributable to this period. However, Woolley found a group of graves on the eastern edge of the royal cemetery, close to the later royal graves of the Ur III Dynasty, which he thought represented a group intermediate in style between those of the First Dynasty and those of Sargonid times. There are fifteen graves in this group: five are shaft graves, laid out in a row, each containing multiple burials. Woolley attributed both the shaft graves and the single graves to the Second Dynasty of Ur, as he called it, in order to stress the intermediate nature of the graves and their contents. The evidence for dating is rather contradictory, as some of the tombs contain features built of the plano-convex bricks so typical of the Early Dynastic period (but see p. 79). The jewellery, by contrast, is Sargonid in style, and the cylinder seals found in the graves range from EDIII combat scenes to Ur III presentation scenes of the late third millennium. One especially interesting find was associated with the shaft of grave 1487. This was a circular stamp seal, of the type found in the Indus valley, with an inscription in Indus characters above the figure of a bull. Its dating is not certain: it was found in a very disturbed area, and it may not belong to the same level as the graves.

Whatever its precise date, it underlines again the importance of the city port of Ur, whose two harbours saw heavy incoming traffic from the Persian Gulf and the Indian Ocean.

We now know, from excavations at other sites, that plano-convex bricks continued in use into the early Agade period. There is also the possibility that the bricks were reused (perhaps there were bricks left over after the endless renovation and remodelling of the ziggurat complex and they were used up by the builders of this group of shaft graves). Finally, it is possible that this shape of brick had some special significance and that they were newly made specifically for the graves. The presence of plano-convex brick is not enough on its own to attribute the graves to the Early Dynastic period. We do, however, have a *terminus ante quem* for them, as the shafts were cut by the digging of some of the Third Dynasty graves, and they must therefore predate them.

One feature unique to this group of five graves is the presence in the shafts of low walls at right angles to the side of the shafts, and usually built of plano-convex bricks. In the best-preserved example in PG1487, there are two niches in the wall, one above the other, facing in opposite directions. Each has a low pedestal in it and it appears that offerings were made in front of them. The evidence from the shaft graves suggests that the burial ritual here was slightly different from that in the rest of the cemetery. First, there is the evidence of the niches; then, most of the bodies were found in coffins and, in PG1487, three children were buried. Another child was found in PG1845. Child burials are very unusual in the rest of the cemetery. Another unusual burial was found in PG1850, where a parcel of disarticulated bones was buried (burial 7). Nor is it entirely clear from the published sections of the shaft graves if the multiple burials are all contemporaneous, as in the royal cemetery. There is some evidence that they are not, as the grave pits tend to overlie each other, suggesting that some time had elapsed since the lower, earlier interment. Given these slightly unusual features, it is tempting to suggest that these are the burials of a discrete group of people, as were the burnt graves described in Chapter 4, and that they represent prosperous family or kin groups who may have reused them over quite a long period of time. This would also explain the range of dates noted for the cylinder seals. Ur, as a major trading port and economic hub, was undoubtedly home to a wide variety of people of different origins over a long period of time.

The final group of graves to be described here comes from the area of the royal cemetery and was attributed by Woolley to the Sargonid period – the period of Sargon of Agade and his successors. There were more than four hundred of them; they showed no marked changes from those of the earlier periods, but were noticeably less rich, and there is no evidence for multiple burials in a single grave, as in the royal graves. The lack of such graves may be due to Ur's new status as a vassal of Agade rather than an independent city state. The evidence does not allow us to say with certainty that human sacrifice – if that is what it was – no longer occurred. We can, however, see minor changes in the jewellery and quite major ones in the style of the cylinder seals and the metalwork. The men no longer wear the beads and rings of the Early Dynastic headdresses, but, instead, have a small oval gold plaque worn on the forehead and held in place by gold ribbons. Women, too, wear this type of headdress rather than the more exuberant examples from the earlier period. In general, there seems to be less gold and silver available and smaller amounts of exotic foreign stones like lapis and carnelian to make into beads and pendants. This relative poverty may again be attributable to Ur's new dependent status rather than to a general lack of prosperity in the Agade period, although the constant wars of Sargon and his immediate successors must have drained resources away from the centre.

It is possible that this proposed pressure on resources explains the predominance in these graves of hammered axes and daggers in simple shapes, made of copper rather than cast in tin or arsenical copper. The weapons in the earlier graves tend to be far better made, cast in various alloys and sometimes decorated with precious metals. Nor is there anything in these graves to suggest the skill shown in the manufacture of the jewellery of the lady Puabi, for example. A second explanation could be that the endless wars had disrupted the trade routes and that copper, tin, lapis and so on were no longer so freely available. A third possibility is that special non-functional items were made especially for burials so that important resources were not squandered on the dead. The hammered axes would have been much less effective than their cast predecessors.

By the middle of the Agade period, by the time of Naram-Sin, the seals are quite distinctive in style, although some of the themes of the earlier third millennium persist (Fig. 6.iii). Earlier than this, it is quite difficult to distinguish the early Agade examples from those of the later Early Dynastic period, as their stylistic development seems to have been gradual. The most fashionable theme to persist is the combat scene, which is transformed in its composition and by the treatment of the figures. The groups comprising the scene are now well spaced and almost heraldic in the way some of them frame an inscription, but

6.iii Agade seal by Tessa Rickards

they lack some of the vigour of the earlier examples. The individual figures are treated in a hyper-realistic manner, with bulging muscles and elaborately curled hair. Many of the protagonists are still animals – lions and bulls, for example – and the human-headed bull remains popular. In addition, there is a hero figure who is usually shown full face with three tightly curled locks of hair on each side of his face, and wearing only a triple belt. Another addition to the repertoire is the Indian zebu or humped bull. The banquet scene becomes rare and then disappears, but the presentation scene is found more often, with humans being presented to gods, or to other important humans; by the succeeding Ur III period, this becomes almost the only design we find.

An innovation of the Agade period is the introduction of scenes that appear to show stories and myths associated with the gods. We see the sun god, for example, rising up from between two mountains to begin his daily journey. We see Ishtar, the goddess of war, her shoulders bristling with weapons and Ea/Enki, god of sweet and salt water and friend to man, sitting in his watery home with fish swimming in the streams of water that flow from his shoulders. We cannot always identify the myths and stories from which the incidents are taken. An exception is the story of the Anzu bird that stole the tablets of destiny from Enlil, and was eventually brought as a captive before the great gods for punishment. The distinctive naturalism of the Agade seals is reflected in other fields as well – especially, perhaps, in some superb pieces of decorative metalwork. We have the head, thought to be that of Sargon himself, and the seated figure of a naked young man. Unfortunately, this only survives from the waist down. Both these magnificent pieces are made of almost pure copper that is notoriously difficult to cast and yet here achieve a remarkable degree of naturalism.

As we have seen earlier, even the most able of the Agade rulers were plagued with revolts. Under the successors of Naram-Sin these problems were made worse by what seems to have been a deteriorating economic situation and raids by unfriendly tribes, who swarmed down from the Zagros mountains in the east, from Elam in south-western Iran and from the desert in the west. The two most frequently named groups are called the Guti in the east and the Amorites in the west. The Guti had the most immediate impact, although, by the end of the third millennium the Amorites were increasingly numerous and increasingly influential with a number of cities ruled by people with Amorite names. After the death of the last Sargonid king, Šar-kali-Šarri (the letter Š is pronounced SH), a period of chaos ensued, for about three years. During this time, the Sumerian King List asks plaintively, 'Who was king and who was not king?' The Guti were then able to take over much of the plain and establish themselves as 'kings'. It is not clear how much territory they actually controlled or for how long they controlled it. The most recent interpretation of the rather skimpy evidence suggests it may have been as little as forty or fifty years.

During this time, some of the great cities of the plain may not have been conquered at all, or may have rapidly broken loose from Gutian control. At Lagash, for example, the names of a number of governors from this period have been found, and at least one of them, called Ur-Bau, was influential enough to be able to have his daughter appointed as high priestess at Ur under the cult name of Enannepadda. (This was the prestigious post once held by Enheduanna, under Sargon, and the appointment tended to be in the hands of the ruler.) Ur-Bau was succeeded by three sons-in-law, of whom the last, Gudea, is the best known, owing to a large number of statues of him. These are mainly in black diorite. They were excavated from a temple in Lagash, and are now in the Louvre Museum in Paris. After Gudea, the history again becomes very confused, but it seems likely that a king of Uruk called Utuhegel, who may have been a younger contemporary of Gudea, chased out the invaders and took control of several of the old city states, including Ur. He seems to have made a man called Ur-Nammu, who may have been a relative, governor of Ur, and it is Ur-Nammu who breaks away from Uruk and founds the Third Dynasty of Ur. He oversaw the beginning of what was arguably the city's most prosperous and important period, which lasted just over a century.

Imperial Ur: The Public Face

At the end of the last chapter, we saw how Ur-Nammu, initially a governor of Ur under Utuhegel of Uruk, broke away around 2100 BC and established himself as an independent ruler, although the close ties with Uruk were to continue. Not content with independence, he swiftly brought many of the major cities of the south under his control, apparently by a skilful mix of negotiation and cajoling. Only in the case of Lagash, and perhaps Uruk itself, was he forced to resort to force. He was a remarkable man, for, as well as being an effective soldier, he was a great builder and an excellent administrator, setting about the reform and centralization of the bureaucracy. He ruled for 18 years, and founded a dynasty that was to last more than a century. He apparently died in battle, but in spite of this – so often a recipe for political disaster – he was succeeded by his son Shulgi, who proved to be just as effective a ruler, consolidating many of his father's reforms and showing that he, too, was an energetic and innovative builder. The dynasty they founded was arguably the political high point in the life of the city of Ur, and some would claim that the city was the capital of the first empire in Mesopotamia whose power extended to the Zagros Mountains in the east and northwards to Sippar, to the west of Baghdad and up the Euphrates towards Mari.

The city of Ur was to be the capital throughout the dynasty, and each ruler in turn built within its sacred temenos, the religious enclosure dedicated to

Kings of the Ur III Dynasty (Middle chronology, the most commonly used one after N. Brisch)

Ur-Nammu	2112–2094 BC
Shulgi/Dungi	2095–2046 BC
Amar-Sin/Bursin	2045–2037 BC
Shū-Sîn	2036–2028 BC
Ibbi-Sîn	2027–2004 BC

the moon god Nannar. Ur-Nammu can claim the credit for starting to build the great ziggurat, parts of which are still visible today, and it remains a potent symbol of the power and prosperity of the period. This or one of the other ziggurats built by Ur-Nammu at Uruk, Eridu and Nippur is generally thought have been the origin of the biblical story of the Tower of Babel, although the ziggurat at Babylon itself is also a contender. Before the ziggurats of the Ur III period, there had been other 'high terraces' crowned with temples, but there is no clear evidence for the genuine three-tiered structure earlier than this. There are a couple of contenders at Kish, whose status remains uncertain, as they were excavated many years ago and have never been properly published. There is also evidence for a plano-convex brick structure of some kind within the Ur-Nammu ziggurat. There has been much discussion of the meaning of these huge buildings, effectively man-made mountains, perhaps intended to reach closer to the heavens where the gods had their dwellings, so that the prayers offered on their summit did not have so far to go. Each was named by its builder and often includes the designation 'mountain'.

The earliest work on clearing the rubbish from the ziggurat at Ur was done by J. E. Taylor in the mid-nineteenth century. Towards the end of the century, an American team began work, but quickly became disillusioned by the size of the challenge. Woolley notes that it was a formidable undertaking, requiring the removal of thousands of tons of rubble before the shape and size of the original could be reconstructed with some certainty. The attempt was further complicated by the repairs and additions of later rulers which, initially, were not always recognized.

Now partially restored by Iraqi archaeologists, the Ur ziggurat and its associated buildings stand in the northern half of the walled city (Fig. 1.ii). The ziggurat itself lies in a smaller enclosure in the north-western corner of the raised sacred enclosure, dominating the town below. Its corners are oriented to the points of the compass, as tradition required. Other buildings inside the temenos include various subsidiary temples; the palace and chapels of the high priestess; the treasury of the god; and a poorly preserved building, which may be the remains of the ruler's palace. It is not even clear if this building was inside the sacred area or just outside it. Finally, close to the earlier Early Dynastic and Agade graveyards, and just outside the temenos wall, we find the tombs built by the Third Dynasty kings.

The ziggurat complex, composed of all these different buildings, was entered up a short flight of steps on its north-eastern side, through the wall of the lower court of Nannar, which was 1.7 metres lower than the ziggurat terrace itself.

7.i The Ziggurat of Ur-Nammu. Reconstruction © British Museum

The court was surrounded by what were probably storerooms, and there were a number of ritual installations in the court, mostly offering places and statue bases – some going back to the Early Dynastic period. An elaborate double gate on the side opposite the steps up to the temenos gave access to the outer world. The thick walls of the court would have offered a serious challenge to any enemy, and Woolley thought that they might have served as the final line of defence. All the structures were built of mud brick, often protected by an outer skin of baked brick, more than 2 metres thick, and set in bitumen mortar. The baked brick skin protected the much more vulnerable unbaked bricks from the elements. Helpfully, some of the bricks were stamped with the name of the king who had commissioned them; so, too, were foundation nails driven into the brickwork. Sometimes we find foundation figures, usually in the shape of a man carrying a basket of bricks on his head, and these, too, often have the name of the builder inscribed on them.

The ziggurat is composed of three superimposed stages. Each one diminishes in size, like wedding-cake tiers. The lowest stage measures about 60 metres by 45 metres and is about 15 metres high in the centre. It was built of a solid mass of brick and proved extremely difficult to plan correctly because none of the lines were straight. It was impossible to see from one corner to another along the base of the structure because of the bowing of the walls; there was also a considerable batter in the vertical plane. Initially, Woolley thought that these features were due to a deliberate attempt to trick the eye into believing the lines were straight, by using the Greek device known as *entasis*. However, he changed his mind and finally suggested that the bulges were due to subsidence. The outer face of the ziggurat is decorated with buttresses and recesses. Small rectangular holes full of broken pottery penetrated deep into the core of the building. Most scholars see them as drainage holes, allowing moisture to escape from the centre of the great terrace, but Woolley himself was determined that they drained the lower terrace. He suggested that it was originally planted with trees to reinforce the impression of the ziggurat as a great mountain. There is certainly provision for drawing water up on to the terrace, but it seems rather doubtful that trees would have survived the broiling sun of a Mesopotamian summer without shelter.

The surface of the first stage is still reached by a triple staircase on the south-east face of the terrace. Two stairs of 100 steps each were attached to its face, one running approximately northwards and the other southwards, while the third ran up between them at right angles to the other two. It is possible that there were small temples in the angles between the central stair and the ones running up the face of the ziggurat on each side of it. All three stairs met just below the level of the terrace and the junction may have been covered with some sort of dome, as seen in the reconstructions. It seems as if the level of the terrace surface was as much as 3 metres higher in the centre than at the corners, and that the two levels were linked by a single flight of steps. The second stage is not preserved to its full height, as it was levelled by Nabonidus in the Neo-Babylonian period. It is estimated to have been about 5.7 metres above stage 1.

The surface of the Ur-Nammu second stage has mostly been destroyed, but there is one feature here not found on the lower stage. A small room was uncovered, built against the south-east face of the ziggurat, whose floor was covered with little copper figures of flies, crescents and boats. Woolley considered that these might represent charms, either offered by supplicants or alternatively sold to them. Perhaps they were like the pilgrim tokens bought in the Middle Ages, to bring good luck and divine protection after a visit to a pilgrimage site.

The third storey has vanished down to its foundations because of later building and erosion, so we can more or less establish its dimensions (20 m x 11.30 m), but nothing else. A small shrine is reconstructed as standing on it, in part as the result of Herodotus's account of the ziggurat at Babylon over a millennium later. He claimed that the shrine on top of the ziggurat contained golden furniture, and that a priestess slept there. The god was also believed to sleep there. Herodotus had an eye for a good story and sometimes let his enthusiasm run away with him, so we cannot be sure of the accuracy of his account. It is also possible that there was no shrine, but, instead, altars for making sacrifices. Sadly, all the other surviving ziggurats are also heavily eroded and it seems unlikely that we will ever know what, if anything, stood on the top stage. With or without a shrine, it must have been an awe-inspiring sight, and a useful landmark visible from great distances in the flat countryside. It was also a clear statement of the devotion and wealth of its builders.

The inner court around the ziggurat was surrounded by a wall with small intramural rooms on three sides. A monumental gate, where justice was dispensed (known later as the *Edublalmah*), was found in the south wall, and it seems that it already existed in the Ur III period. A second gate may also have been present in the eastern corner of the court, while to the north-west there lay traces of a shrine to Nannar and a cluster of smaller rooms. These are probably all that remains of the kitchen temple where the food for the god was prepared. Much later, we know that the Ningal temple, dedicated to Nannar's wife, lay in the south-east of the enclosure and it may already have been present here, although there is no evidence for it at this period. A well and a fine cistern were the only constructions recovered here.

It was in and around the *Edublalmah* that pieces of one of the most interesting artefacts of the Ur III period were found lying below building remains of the Kassite period of the mid-second millennium (Fig. 7.11). Although some pieces were still missing, when fitted together they formed a stela showing a king, probably Ur-Nammu, being presented to the moon god, the divine ruler of Ur. The attribution to Ur-Nammu is based on an inscription on the stela, listing a number of canals which he is known to have built. His name also occurs on a fragment of a skirt. Unfortunately, this cannot even be shown to be definitely part of the stela. It was made of a fine-grained stone, and, as restored, is about 3 metres high and 1.54 metres wide at the base, and slightly smaller at the top, which was rounded. It had originally been carved on both sides and the design was divided into registers, as in the earlier stelae of the ED III period. Regrettably, the design is incomplete, especially on one side, where weathering has caused the stone to flake away in a number of places. The pieces were sent to Philadelphia for treatment and reconstruction and it was assumed that the better-preserved face was the front of the monument.

The initial reconstruction showed the 'front' as having five registers. The uppermost was about twice the height of the lower ones. It shows the ruler standing under a large crescent moon, which encloses an elaborate star. He has one arm raised in greeting before a seated deity. Only the horned helmet, the

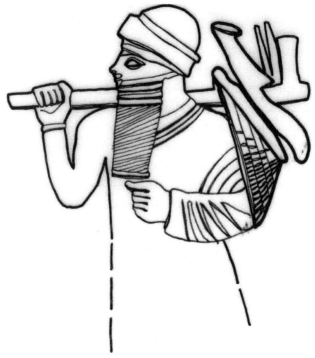

7.ii Figure of Ur-Nammu from his stela

feet of the god and the base of the throne are preserved. A second pair of feet can be seen dangling below where the lap of the god would have been. It has always been assumed that the deity was the moon god, with a smaller deity or a child seated on his lap, but it seems possible that this is Ningal, Nannar's wife, with a child on her lap. Kings of the time often claim to have been breast-fed by a goddess, so could the child have been Ur-Nammu himself, or Shulgi his son? Such a scene would have been an impressive piece of propaganda for the regime. Traces of two protective goddesses pouring life-giving water can be seen floating above the king.

The second register is the best preserved. In the centre, two figures stand back to back, each attended by a second figure which is preserved only from shoulder-level down, so we cannot be sure if this is a human attendant or an interceding goddess with her hands raised. The king figure on the right pours a libation into a palm tree in a vase, which stands in front of a seated god who holds out the so-called rod and line, the traditional symbols of kingship. They probably represent the tools of the surveyor for measuring plans and angles, as temple building and restoration were vital obligations on the ruler. The figure facing left is also pouring a libation on to an identical palm tree, but this time it stands in front of a seated goddess. We can guess that this is the divine couple Nannar and Ningal.

Only a small part of the third register is preserved, and it shows the ruler (preceded by a deity) carrying a hod with builder's tools in it, obviously on his way to start building a temple, or perhaps the ziggurat itself. Behind him, a servant supports some of the weight of the hod so the king did not have to overexert himself! The last two registers are very fragmentary, but seem to show the building works in progress. A man carrying bricks or soil on his head and a ladder leaning against the side of a building are almost all that remain.

The badly weathered side (conventionally referred to as the reverse of the stela), is impossible to recreate in full, as we only have disconnected bits, the majority of which seem to show religious ceremonies of various sorts. At the top, the remains of the flying goddesses can be seen, again pouring out the water of life over a figure of the king, but the rest of the scene is lost. Another piece shows a seated figure on a dais wearing a flounced robe, while a naked figure stands on a step below him, holding what might be a fly-whisk and a towel. A second figure in a long robe with a shaved head (so probably a priest) has his back turned to the seated figure, and holds out a towel to a bearded figure in front of him. This might be the king, or – as has recently been suggested – a wrestler. Wrestling was a popular sport at some major festivals, and this would explain the curious position of the bearded figure's (or someone else's) arm. Another piece of the stela shows two men, one with tightly curled hair, playing what looks like a big drum that is as tall as they are. There is also a scene of sacrifice, where a man (the head is missing) is preparing to sacrifice a bull, with his foot on its muzzle, while another figure holds a smaller, headless animal whose blood is pouring out in front of a broken figure standing on a small plinth. Behind this figure, the legs of another man can be seen, along with some peculiar symbols that could be a depiction of trees and landscape. A final fragment probably comes from a different stela and depicts a man with curly hair, milking a cow. The stela is of great interest not only for the scenes it represents, but also because it demonstrates a stylistic mixture. Links with the Early Dynastic period are suggested by its division into registers. Typical of the Agade period is its more naturalistic treatment of the figures, while a new set of themes are entirely its own.

A few pieces of statues in the round were also found, although none of them were in their original position so it is difficult to date them precisely. It is, in fact, extremely difficult to distinguish on stylistic grounds alone between the art of

Gudea of Lagash and that of the early Ur rulers, or between that of the late Ur III period and examples belonging to the succeeding Isin-Larsa period. After restoration, the most complete statue recovered shows a woman in a flounced dress sitting on an elaborate stool. There is a long inscription dedicating the statue to Ningal and stating that it was dedicated by the lady Enanatuma, daughter of the king of Isin, who was appointed high priestess when her father came to power. She also rebuilt the *Gigparku* after it had been destroyed by the Elamites. It is not clear if the statue represents the goddess or the donor. Another rather lumpen statue of black stone shows a goddess seated on a throne with the figure of a goose below it. The goose was usually found as the symbol of the goddess of healing, so the figure may be that of Bau or Gula. Woolley illustrates parts of several other statues, but, apart from most of a fine female head in white stone with inlaid eyes, they tell us very little about the art of the period.

After the ziggurat itself and its subsidiary buildings, the next most important building lies outside the inner enclosure, to the south-east of it, but inside the temenos. Inscriptions name it as the *Gigparku* (see plan 1.ii), the official residence of the high priestess of the moon god, the *entu*. There are traces of an earlier building enclosed within the platform on which the Ur III *Gigparku* was built. Sadly, not enough of the walls survive to be able to reconstruct the earlier plan, and all we can say is that it was on a different alignment to the Ur III building, whose corners were correctly oriented to the points of the compass. We have already seen that the position of high priestess was an important one, at least from the Early Dynastic period onwards, so it is no surprise to find the impressive remnants of her official residence. We also know that the post was held by Enheduanna, the daughter of Sargon of Agade. It should be remembered that in addition to her duties as a priestess, the *entu* was also expected to run a major estate and to keep her palace in good repair.

The building was about 70 metres square, with thick, buttressed walls and only two entrances, so that it must have been easy to defend if necessary. The building divides into two main halves separated by a corridor, giving access from one half to the other through a single door.

The sector nearer the ziggurat (section A) housed the priestess's living quarters and elaborate private chapel, as well as a curious unit of three parallel rooms, isolated by a surrounding passage and accessed from the central corridor (B6/7/8). In the middle room of the three, Woolley found three round-topped stelae, badly defaced, but with the name of Amar-Sin, Shulgi's successor, and a dedication to the goddess Ningal still legible. Woolley thought they had probably been moved there for storage, possibly having stood originally in the courtyard of the large temple. The complex looks like a kind of treasury, isolated as it is by its passage (B5) around three sides. It may also have been a storage area for the great kitchens on the other side of the corridor. To the west, beyond the central unit, was a double shrine (B1/2), where two niches suggest the worship of a pair of gods, but there is no evidence to suggest who they may have been.

To the east of the storage area lay a badly damaged complex of small rooms with tombs below them, all empty, having been badly robbed. Woolley thought they might have been the graves of previous priestesses (B15/26). We know from tablets retrieved from another of the great buildings in the temenos, the *Enunmah,* that food offerings were routinely made to the dead *entus* in the succeeding Isin-Larsa period, and this seems to have been the continuation of a long-established tradition.

As we have seen, the great kitchen (C32/4) was located just the other side of the dividing corridor from the storage area, and it must, for its time, have had all modern conveniences! There were two fireplaces 'for heating water' (and for roasting perhaps?), a cylindrical bread oven or *tannur*, and a cooking range with two fireboxes and small holes in its flat upper surface on which to sit the pots. A large chopping block of brick still had the knife marks visible on its surface, and a metal ring set in the floor may have been where beasts were tied for slaughter, or where the rope for pulling water from the well was anchored. There was a well, and a bitumen-lined tank for water storage. It is not difficult to imagine a retinue of cooks scurrying about here as they put together lavish meals. This is the only set of rooms to have access to both halves of the building, so it probably provided food both for the deity and for the high priestess and her retinue.

The half of the complex further from the ziggurat (section C) housed a temple, built, as usual, round a large courtyard. The walls of this temple were unusually well preserved, as, when the building was destroyed by invading Elamites at the end of the Ur III period, the walls fell inwards, filling up the rooms. When the Isin-Larsa Dynasty began the work of restoring these sacred buildings, they simply erected a platform over the rubble of the walls and built on that, preserving the earlier remains for Woolley to find. The main access to the temple courtyard is from the temenos, with a second from section A of the *Gigparku,* although this was a rather complicated and circuitous route. The area had been violently destroyed by Babylonian troops and a thick layer of ash had helped to preserve many objects originally dedicated to the temple. The plaque of Enheduanna was found here, as were the two female statues, one probably representing a goddess of healing such as Bau or Gula, described above. There were also pieces of many stone bowls in the debris, dedicated to the temple over the years, some inscribed with the names of the donors. One had the name of Naram-Sin of Agade on it and was then dedicated (or rededicated?) by one of Shulgi's daughters. A brick base in the courtyard still held fragments of a black stone stela, which listed the victories of Hammurabi of Babylon, one of the last kings to worship in the temple before its destruction by his son, Samsu-iluna.

The plan of the temple differed in one important respect from earlier temples. Its inner and outer shrines are parallel to each other, and the statue of the god originally stood in a niche in the long wall of the inner shrine (C20/27). This position meant that it was visible from the courtyard, which gave access to the shrine. In earlier temples, the divine statue is usually placed on the short wall, and is hidden from public view by a bent axis approach. It is interesting to speculate that this change in the plan of the temple reflects ideological change too. Could it reflect the greater accessibility to the gods, which may have been linked to the deification of all but the first ruler of the dynasty? A small room to the south of the niche for the statue had nothing in it but a large platform half-filling the space (C28). Woolley suggested that this was where the sacred marriage took place between the god and the priestess. This remains a romantic, but controversial theory, with little to support it. There were a number of small rooms round the courtyard, and those to the south probably housed the temple scribes and various other servants of the goddess, judging from the tablets found there in the Isin-Larsa reconstruction. The temple was responsible for large estates, and, very likely, for the quasi-industrial production of cloth as well, so there must have been a bureaucracy in place to cope with business matters on behalf of the high priestess. A weaver's pit was found in the same range of rooms, but this was production on a household level, presumably to supply the god and her servants with the materials for their clothing.

The next building to consider is probably one of the oldest foundations within the temenos, apart from the ziggurat itself. It is called the *Enunmah*, loosely translated as the House of Plenty. It seems to have served as the store for many of the precious votive offerings brought to the temple, and, to judge from the many tablets found in the rubble, also for the tithes from the tenant farmers. In addition, it was the office where rations were issued to temple workers. It lies in the right angle made where the south-east wall of the court of Nannar meets the wall of the ziggurat enclosure. Its corners are oriented to the points of the compass and it stands on a terrace formed by enclosing the ruinous walls of earlier buildings, some of which are built of mid-third-millennium plano-convex brick. Very little, except for the foundations, remains of Ur-Nammu's building either and the plan is incomplete, but it seems to have been square: its walls measured about 57 metres and were ornamented with the usual buttresses and recesses. Its original entrance probably lay on the north-west wall, facing the court of Nannar, but that area is very disturbed.

The most remarkable feature of the plan is a small unit of five rooms that forms the core of the building, the rest of which is made up of long rectangular magazines for storage. This unit is isolated from the rest of the building by a passage. It has some similarity to the possible storage unit in section B of the *Gigparku* (see above) which contained storage rooms and was isolated by a passage, distancing it from the rest of the building. It is suggested that the unit of five rooms in the *Enunmah* is a double shrine with service rooms and a common courtyard. (A double temple was also found next to the *Gigparku* unit.) It is only in the time of Nebuchadnezzar that a double shrine can be definitely identified here; the status of the rooms in earlier times is unclear, and they could well have been a secure treasury to house the many precious offerings made to the temple of the moon god. Below the floors of several of the rooms (10–13), masses of broken stone vases and tablets were found dating back to the time of Sargon of Agade. This strengthens the case for the longevity of the building, as many of the fragments were inscribed with the names of the royal donors, whose dates are known. The fragments were probably offerings made to the god, and were presumably thought too important and too sacred to be thrown away.

The penultimate building to be considered raises more questions than answers. It is located south-east of the *Gigparku* and south of the *Enunmah,* but separated from them by an earth bank. It is not even clear if it was inside or outside the temenos wall, which may have been extended in order to include it. Woolley thought it was inside, but this is far from clear. It divides into two unequal sections, the upper half apparently formal rooms and the other half domestic, but the plan is incomplete and even the location of the entrance is not certain. The north and west corners, as restored in Woolley's plan, are largely hypothetical and, in addition, some scholars suggest that the building had a second floor over all but the largest 'courtyard', so many questions remain to be answered. We do know that its name was the *E-HurSag* (the house of the mountain) and that it was built in part by Ur-Nammu, whose bricks are found in the walls, and probably finished by his son Shulgi, whose name is found on the baked bricks of the pavements and whose inscription says that he built 'His beloved house, the *E-HurSag'*. The walls were well built of burnt brick set in bitumen mortar, on mud-brick foundations, and the plan was correctly oriented with the corners of the building to the points of the compass. Foundation deposits were discovered under the south and east corners of the building and included copper figures of a man, probably the ruler, carrying a basket of bricks on his head and blank tablets of steatite, a shiny black stone. A third deposit is thought to have been found during restoration work by Iraqi archaeologists. Such votive deposits are usually inscribed with the name of the builder, but, sadly, not in this case.

Woolley interpreted the building as the palace of the kings of Ur, partly because the Shulgi building inscriptions refer to it as 'His (Shulgi's) beloved house', but not everyone is in agreement. Its location is not in favour of this identification, as, if we look at other near-contemporaneous palaces, they are not built inside the sacred enclosure, but seem to be deliberately placed well away from it. At Uruk, the Sinkashid palace is positioned on the city wall, west of the Anu ziggurat, and below it are the fragmentary remains of an earlier Ur III palace, apparently in the same position. The slightly later palace of Nur-Adad at Larsa is also positioned well away from the main temple and on the opposite side of what may be a city gate. The same is true at Mashkan-Shapir, a town of Old Babylonian date and so slightly younger than the Ur building. This deliberate distancing of palace and temple might reflect a changing view of the relationship between what could loosely be called church and state.

Could the *Ehursag* perhaps be the offices and living quarters of some of the most important temple administrators, rather than the home of the ruler? The more formal half of the building could be where people came to present petitions, claim rations, and perhaps pay their dues, while the rest of the palace could be seen as living quarters for the officials. It is odd that there do not seem to be offices within the temenos, apart from a couple of small rooms in the *Gigparku* and the storage rooms around the court of Nannar, although we know from the tablets that the temple was an extremely important economic force in the community, overseeing large amounts of land. It was also involved in the commercial production of cloth, and in trading ventures, both within Mesopotamia and with lands further away. It would be reasonable to expect to find more evidence of such important administrative activities.

The final complex of buildings is a group of three tombs, which were terraced into the area just outside the temenos on the east side, close to the area of the EDIII graves. They were built by Shulgi and Amar-Sin, according to the inscriptions on the bricks, and Woolley was convinced that they were the royal tombs of the dynasty. If he is correct, then they are the most powerful statement we have seen yet of the worship of the divine kings of the dynasty (Fig. 7.iii).

Each tomb is built on the same plan as the private houses (discussed in the

7.iii Photo of entrance to Shulgi tomb © Dr Jane Moon

next chapter) and is equipped with the most elaborate provision for making offerings. To judge from the runnels and cup-marks found on the altars, the offerings included food, drink, and the burning of resins or oils as incense. These mortuary chapels lie above the vaulted tomb chambers, which were apparently built before the superstructure, inserted into a huge pit with a baked brick floor, initially with a temporary superstructure until the chapels above were complete.

The complex built by Shulgi is the central one, and the most elaborate. It is built largely of expensive baked brick, with hugely thick walls correctly oriented, and decorated externally with buttresses and recesses. The corners of the building are carefully rounded. The chapel was entered through a monumental door on the north-east wall, which led into a lobby. In turn, this gave on to the central court, where the first of the altars was found against the south-west wall. There was also a pillar set in the west wall by the entrance to room 7. Similar altars and pillars can be seen in the chapels belonging to some of the private houses of Ur III date (see Chapter 8). The building had been thoroughly looted, but enough remained to show that fragments of gold leaf had originally covered some of the doors, and traces of elaborate inlay in gold, lapis and agate, including a number of tiny gold stars, were also found in some of the rooms, indicating that the décor in its heyday must have been sumptuous. The paved courtyard was surrounded by rooms: a double row on the west, and single rows elsewhere. The two most important rooms were those on the south-west wall. Room 5 (see plan 1.ii) had altars covered with gold for burnt offerings, liquids and incense. It lay above tomb 2, while the adjacent room 6, whose floor lay 2 metres above that of room 5, lay above tomb 1, the larger of the two.

The tombs themselves were large corbel-vaulted structures, but it looks as if the original floor had been badly executed and a second floor had to be hastily inserted at a higher level. The tombs were originally approached by a flight of steps from room 7 which ran down to a landing. From there, two further flights of steps ran to the east and west, giving access to the tombs themselves. The lower stairs, too, were covered with a corbel vault, and once they had been completed, construction seems to have been halted while various further rituals were carried out. Finally, the stairs linking the landing to room 7 were completed, and then the whole was back-filled. When the fill was removed from the stairs, it became obvious that both tombs had been robbed, a small hole having been dug through the blocking of their doors. This must have happened just before the infilling of the stairs to the graves which covered up the evidence of this sacrilege. All that remained of the original contents of the tombs were bones, both human and animal, and a few pieces of pottery. It is not clear how many people were buried, or what the distinction was between those in tomb 1 and those in tomb 2. There are the scattered remains of seven or eight people (including at least one woman and one child). It seems likely that the burials were simultaneous, as it would have been very difficult to get into the tombs once the stairs had been buried. Were these people members of the royal family or the royal court, or sacrificial victims reminiscent of the Early Dynastic royal burials? Regrettably, this is another question that we shall probably never be able to answer.

A little light is shed by two literary compositions, both written sometime after the events they purport to describe. As literary works, they cannot be assumed to be accurate depictions of the funeral rites of the late third millennium. However, the picture they paint is interesting. The first is called 'The Death of Ur-Namma'. This poem describes how the king was brought back to his palace to die; he then descends to the Underworld and there throws a sumptuous feast and gives magnificent gifts to the more important gods. They are so pleased with the presents that they decree that he shall have his own palace and sit alongside Gilgamesh as a divine judge for all eternity. Presumably, the gifts were placed in the tomb with the king, and they are very reminiscent of the goods found in the earlier royal tombs, which included many rich and beautiful objects. A second poem describes the death of Gilgamesh* and tells how his family and his court descend into his tomb carrying a dazzling array of gifts for the gods of the Underworld. The tomb is then sealed and the journey to the land of the dead begins. It is possible that these descriptions are a fictionalized version of the events that took place in our royal tombs.

The other two tombs in the complex are similar in plan to that of Shulgi. The one attributed to Amar-Sin lies to the south-east and is well built, but rather smaller. The one to the north-west, however, seems to be a later addition to the complex, built with bricks apparently left over from the earlier buildings, and is not so well planned. It is also unusual in having a tomb located under the central court rather than under a chapel. In the main tomb, under room 4, the bones of five women were found, all carrying traces of burning. We can only speculate on who the women were. They may have been royal consorts or daughters, or ladies of the court. In fact, it is very unclear for whom any of the tombs were built. Woolley felt that the Shulgi complex had probably been built by Shulgi for his father Ur-Nammu, but there is no evidence for Ur-Nammu having been deified, so how do we explain the funerary chapels? On Woolley's reasoning, the Amar-Sin complex would have been built for his father Shulgi. The third complex remains unexplained. More recently, it has been suggested that the kings of Ur may not have been buried here at all, but may have been interred in or near to their palace, as was the custom in the Assyrian period. These tombs may have been for the high priests, the governors, or other high officials.

The central temenos, with its impressive and costly buildings, tells us much about the religious and ceremonial heart of the city of Ur. This is concrete propaganda for the ruling dynasty, emphasizing its piety and wealth, as well as the fact that the kings were chosen by the gods as rulers. The buildings' literal and metaphorical centrality, coupled with their rich decorations, goes some way to explain the devastation they suffered when the city fell to the Elamites in around 2000 BC. However, in spite of their importance, they tell us nothing about the lives of the ordinary inhabitants or about the city's thriving commercial activities. For this we need to look elsewhere, and the evidence from the residential areas of the city will be discussed in the next chapter.

---

* In Sumerian the name is written Bilgamesh.

Ur Beyond the Sacred Precinct: Ur III to Isin-Larsa (Early Old Babylonian) Periods*

The magnificent complex of public buildings, described in the last chapter, that formed the heart of the city of Ur was violently destroyed. After a series of disasters including treachery, drought and famine, the Third Dynasty fell to an invading army of Elamites, Gutians and others from the east and north-east. The last king of the dynasty, Ibbi-Sin, was carried off in chains to Elam in about the year 2000 BC. The impact of the destruction was such that it inspired a whole genre of lamentation poems to speak of the horrors the city had endured. The gods were thought to have abandoned their temples and the destruction was portrayed as the end of civilization itself. In practice, however, there seems to have been an element of poetic licence in these lamentations. The archaeological evidence suggests that rebuilding began almost immediately under the dynasties of Isin and Larsa. In turn, these became the new overlords of Ur. Ur was still held in such high esteem that the kings of Isin used the title 'King of Ur'. Not only that, but the extensive area of private housing excavated by Woolley shows little sign of a massive destruction at the end of the third millennium. It seems that ordinary life may have continued, perhaps on a reduced scale, in spite of the disasters, but political glory had gone for ever.

The main, roughly oval mound of the city of Ur measures about 1,200 metres by 800 metres, and the walled centre of the city lay between the Euphrates and a large canal. The site is actually far bigger than just the central mound (see Fig. 1.ii on p. 11). The remains of houses and associated graves can be traced on the surface of a series of mounds for about a mile northwards, although it is not possible to date them exactly without excavation. A metalworking area was

---

* The nomenclature is rather confusing. Older publications talk about the dynasty of Isin, which was followed by the dynasty of Larsa. More recently, some scholars regard these two phases together as the early part of the Old Babylonian period.

also identified from its surface remains. The remains of houses stretch as far as a low-lying, roughly triangular site called Diqdiqqah. This seems to have been an industrial suburb of Ur. Inscribed cones of Ur-Nammu refer to the building of three new canals in this area, and to the refurbishment of an old one. It is suggested that a number of canals, which were important arteries of communication, may have met here, making this a commercial hub. Only a part of the site is preserved and, unfortunately, the rest has been lost to erosion and to agriculture. This means that most of the small finds from the area are without provenance. Many were brought in by Woolley's workmen, who crossed the area on their way to work at Ur: it was his policy to pay *baksheesh* for every find. The finds are of various dates going back to the Agade period, but the majority seem to belong to the early part of the second millennium. There are many terracottas, mostly mass-produced in moulds, and a number of frit objects, all of which may have been made here.

The only surviving building at Diqdiqqah is part of a large fortified structure known as the Treasury of Sin-iddinam, a king of Larsa. Inscriptions on some of the pavement bricks of the building give his name and refer to the building as 'The great and noble abode of treasure', suggesting it may have been some kind of customs office where goods in transit were stored. The attribution to Sin-iddinam is a little uncertain, as similar bricks with the same inscription were found in the ziggurat area and the surplus may have been used later at Diqdiqqah. The remains of the so-called Treasury are extremely impressive and are made up of heavily buttressed walls of burnt brick. The most intact was about forty metres long. The surviving corners are oriented to the corners of the compass, as in all the major public buildings discussed in the last chapter. The north and west corners are preserved, and they, too, are impressively buttressed. Inside, one row of rooms is preserved: a long hall about twenty metres in length, with a smaller room at either end. Two great supports in the shape of Maltese crosses can be seen on the south side of the hall; the excavator suggested they supported a barrel-vaulted roof. Traces of two doorways on the north-west and north-east walls are the only other remains. It looks as if these sidewalls must have been around thirty metres long at least, making this an enormous structure, capable of holding a huge amount of goods.

Ur-Nammu claims in his inscriptions to have built a formidable wall around the main mound of the city, but no trace of it was found, probably because it was thoroughly destroyed by the invaders at the end of the Third Dynasty. Even when there was no wall, the backs of the houses packed side by side along the perimeter of the mound above its sloping sides must have presented a formidable barrier. In addition, temples to Enki and Ningizida (?), both originally built in the time of the Third Dynasty and extensively restored under the last Larsa king, Rim-Sin, stood on the wall and were incorporated into the defences. Here, they presumably provided divine protection, in addition to being a physical barrier. Elsewhere, Warad-Sin, penultimate king of Larsa, built a magnificent defensive bastion and gateway on to the ziggurat terrace. It was decorated with patterns similar to those seen on palm tree trunks after they have been trimmed. This decoration was repeated on a number of other slightly later public buildings at Larsa, and in Assyria to the north. Two harbours can be seen on the north and west of the mound, one on the river and one on the major canal; in fact, the city was probably surrounded by water on three sides, presenting another formidable barrier to attackers. The waterways also underline the importance of trade to Ur's economy. Another large canal ran from the north harbour across the heart of the city. It probably had a number of smaller canals branching off it that brought water to individual households.

Thanks to Woolley's far-sightedness in spreading his excavations outside the central area of the site, we have a good idea of the layout of the town outside the sacred area, and of the structure of the urban landscape – something that is rarely available to us. The most extensive area of housing is in the area known as AH. Measuring approximately 10,000 square metres (Fig. 8.i), it lay about halfway between the sacred precinct and the city wall, to the south-east of the temenos. A smaller area, EM, was excavated between the temenos wall and the west harbour, while a third area, EH, lay just outside the earlier temenos enclosure but inside that of Nebuchadnezzar. A final group of houses called the Mausoleum site were built, as the name suggests, over the Third Dynasty royal graves. This position indicates that they belong to the period of the Larsa kings after the location of the Third Dynasty royal graves had been forgotten. We will concentrate on the AH site, as it is the largest and most diverse of the areas, and the others are similar to it. The EH site is rather different and will be described separately.

The constant rebuilding, visible in all the domestic areas, makes it very difficult to date the individual houses. As houses were modified, torn down and re-erected on the whim of the owner, adjacent houses that are contemporary may be at very different heights in the archaeological record. Dating is made even more difficult because it seems that when a man died, his property, including his house, was divided between his surviving sons. Daughters were also entitled to a share as part of their dowries. This led to constant modifications of the original plan to accommodate the new owners, frequently over a

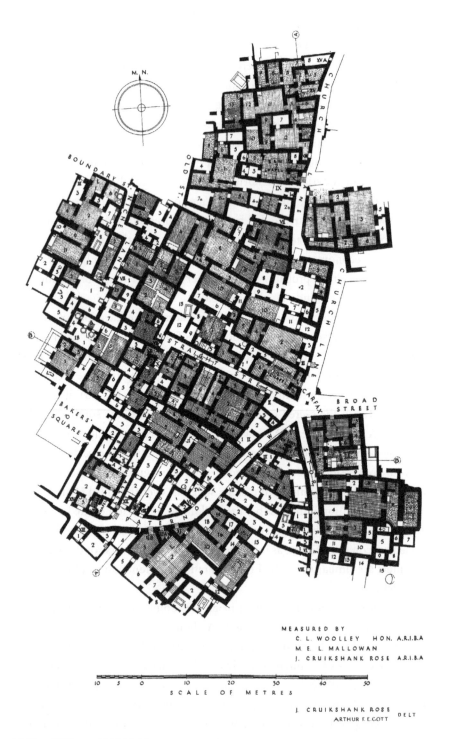

8.i Plan of AH area. © British Museum

short span of time. Even more confusing is the fact that pottery styles – the means by which archaeologists often determine dates – change little in the first 250 years of the second millennium. Except in cases where it is possible to give a more exact date (because of the presence of datable tablets, for example), the area of housing is generally given a blanket date and is referred to as being of Isin-Larsa date, although a few of the houses undoubtedly go back to Ur III, and some are as late as the Old Babylonian period. It is to the Isin-Larsa period that most of the houses in their final phases belonged. As we have seen, the rulers of first Isin and then Larsa each, in turn, absorbed the city of Ur into their fiefdoms and carried out a considerable amount of building and repair work, primarily inside the temenos, to put right some of the destruction caused by the invading Elamites at the end of the Ur III period.

The domestic quarters of the city show little trace of central planning in area AH (see Fig 8.i). Even main roads wander around the houses, sometimes converging on a small open space or square. There were no drainage systems in the roads and, as people seem to have thrown their domestic rubbish out of the front door into the street, the street level rose gradually until it was higher than the floor level inside the buildings. Woolley states that the level in a road he named Paternoster Row rose by more than a metre during the lifetime of house 15. This meant that when it rained, filth would be washed down off the road and into the houses. To prevent this happening, the door sills were gradually built up, course by course, until the doorway was so low that it made entry difficult and a new house had to be built on the dismantled walls of the old one. Smaller lanes branch off the main roads, giving access to groups of houses; in some cases, the smallest of them are thought to have been owned jointly by the houses on either side. Woolley rather charmingly named the roads after roads in Oxford, which he had known when he was a student and later when he worked at the Ashmolean Museum. The 'square' where three roads converged was called Carfax and we also find the aforementioned Paternoster Row, Store Street, New Street and so on. The external corners of the buildings were carefully rounded, to minimize the damage to goods, donkeys and people passing by. The streets are so narrow that carts would not have been able to enter them.

We are lucky to have one or two tablets on which are drawn examples of the ideal house of the period, perhaps for the benefit of apprentice architects or engineers. This was built around an open court with rooms all around it. Air and light come from the central courtyard, and the outside walls present a blank face to the world. Many of the houses at Ur conformed to this ideal in their early stages, before being modified by frequent rebuilding. There is much debate over the presence or absence of an upper floor at Ur; they certainly existed at other cities such as Sippar, where there are textual references to upper floors, but the evidence from Ur is inconclusive. Woolley based his view that they had existed on a single emplacement for a pillar in one of the courtyards. He interpreted this as having been one of four posts supporting a wooden balcony connecting the first-floor rooms, as in the traditional Baghdadi house. There are certainly stairs in many of the houses, but these may have led to the roof rather than to a first floor as, especially in warm weather, the roof, probably shaded by some kind of awning, became an important space for sleeping and working.

The houses were built of mud brick. The more expensive baked brick was used for the outside walls, for 'damp courses', and in areas where water was used. Unbaked bricks were used in less important areas. Some of the doorways were arched and all walls were heavily plastered. The roofs were made of palm trunks, branches, matting and mud plaster: these needed a certain amount of annual renewal, but all the materials were cheap and easily available. There seem to have been a number of different plans in use depending in part on the size of the family and the wealth of the inhabitants. Not all the buildings were domestic. In the AH site some of them, like the small single- or double-roomed units opening directly on to the street, may have been shops, and a number of these can be seen close together on the east side of Baker's Square. One rather grander example is in a house immediately behind the Bazaar chapel (see p. 102), which had a large hatch or window giving on to the street. Explanations for this unique feature are extremely varied, ranging from a fast-food shop to a brothel – the latter interpretation being based on the presence of some erotic clay plaques!

Other non-domestic buildings were the small neighbourhood chapels. They might consist of a courtyard with a single room at the far end, with a niche for the statue of the god on the rear wall, like the Bazaar chapel. The Nin-Shubur chapel is a very unusual triangular shape, dictated by the routes of Paternoster Row and Store Street, with two small rooms at the wide end. A clumsy limestone statue of the goddess was found at the entrance to the chapel. Other more elaborate chapels include what may have been living quarters for the priest, as in the Hendursag and Ram chapels. The Hendursag chapel still had a statue standing in the niche. It was of a smiling, cloaked woman made of white limestone with a row of neatly arranged curls across her forehead (Fig. 8.ii). She has no obvious attributes of divinity and it has been suggested that she might have been a worshipper rather than the goddess herself. A second, rather fierce-looking, dumpy woman wearing the flounced dress of a goddess was found in the courtyard, together with a pillar of coarse-grained limestone with a hollowed-out top 'Like a Holy water stoup', according to Woolley. The sides of the pillar are decorated with crudely carved figures of humans and birds. The style suggests that the pillar may date back to the third millennium. The final statue from this courtyard is made of copper and is of a standing goddess in a flounced dress and horned headdress, perhaps Hendursag herself (?). She was found in the remains of what seems to have been a wooden box. Outside the entrance to the shrine was a painted terracotta relief of a protective deity, probably originally one of two guarding the entrance.

Number 1B Baker's Square was extensively remodelled during its lifetime, and in its last phase contained three kilns and a pile of what was thought to be lime. Originally, it had been a bakery, but in its last phase it saw a change of

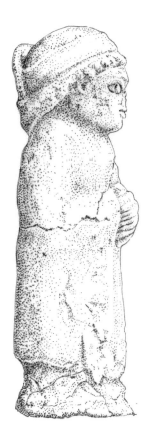

8.ii Statue from the Hendursag chapel by Tessa Rickards

function, and the lime was perhaps being fired to provide the gypsum for the ubiquitous white plaster. One 'hybrid' building at 3 Paternoster Row seems, on the basis of the tablets found in it, to have been a small school with attached schoolmaster's house. Next to it was an unusual building with three entrances, a number of small rooms and an underground storage room. Woolley interpreted this complex as an inn or *khan*. The AH neighbourhood seems to have had all the essential services, with chapels, schools and shops within easy walking distance, and the variety of floor areas in the houses suggests that it was a socially mixed area as well.

Some houses had one courtyard, others two, and the largest type had three. It is very difficult to determine the usage of the rooms round the courtyards as most spaces seem to have been multipurpose. During the day they would be used for sitting and working; then, at night, mats would be brought out for people to sleep on. The large room on the far side of the courtyard from the entrance was probably the main reception area used by both family and visitors. The kitchens can be identified by the ovens and *tannurs* in them, and are generally found opening on to the courtyard, or in it, so that in hot weather the heat generated by cooking was dissipated. A large porous pot was generally placed in a shady corner to keep the water supply for cooking and drinking as cool as possible. Some of the courtyards slope gently towards the centre, where a small tank might be placed to drain off water in the rainy season. One or two of the houses also have lavatories (usually placed adjacent to the stairs). It seems that in some houses the room nearest the entrance could be used as an office, to judge from tablets found in some of them, perhaps so that business could be transacted without inconveniencing the rest of the family. An interesting analysis of 'permeability' (that is to say, rooms that are connected to the outside world, the courtyard or each other) does not suggest that any part of the family group living in a house was segregated. There is no evidence for any sort of harem. However, access to the outside world could be controlled if necessary, especially in the double-courtyard houses, by a small room at the entrance for a door-keeper or porter.

Finally, we find a new feature in the larger houses, which sometimes contain a chapel. Access to this special room was tightly controlled; it tended to be as far from the entrance as possible, and often lay behind the reception room. This may explain why family archives or business documents are sometimes found in chapels, or in small cupboard-type rooms off them, placed there for safety. The chapel was partially roofed and the floor was paved. It usually had a brick altar, a table or offering stand decorated with a pattern of buttresses and recesses moulded in mud plaster (to mimic the exterior of a temple perhaps), and a hearth with a short chimney for burning incense. The vaulted family tomb is found beneath the floor of the chapel or, if there was no chapel, under the floor of another room, or even under the courtyard. The vaults seem to have been opened as necessary to inter adult members of the family, and when the vault was full individuals were placed in clay coffins outside it. The latest interment was placed in the tomb lying on its side with hands in front of its face, often holding a drinking bowl, as in the third-millennium graves. Earlier burials were pushed to the sides to make room for the newcomer. In contrast to the Early Dynastic burials, very few offerings were found in the vaults apart from an individual's personal seal and the drinking bowl. A few clay pots were sometimes found outside the brickwork blocking the door. By contrast, babies and very young children were placed in bowls or little coffins in front of the altar with no grave goods. There seems to have been a feeling that the family should stay together in death as in life, and the presence of your family tomb must have strengthened your claim to the building, if it was ever contested. It is interesting that when a man died it was the duty of the eldest son to look after the graves; he was allocated a larger share of his father's estate to allow him to do this.

Max Mallowan, who worked as Woolley's assistant for a number of years, has a charming description in his memoirs of Woolley showing groups of entranced visitors round the houses. He would apparently say things like: 'Now, take a look at the roof. I know you cannot see it, but we know everything about it that matters.' Mallowan describes him as an incomparable showman who seemed to know the inhabitants of each of the houses personally, and introduced them to his visitors!

The tablets give us the names of some of the inhabitants and indications of their professions. There is evidence for financiers, landowners and various other professions, including a man who provided bread for the central authorities. One of the houses belonged to a man called Ea-Nasir; thanks to the tablets found in it, we know that he was a merchant, working in both the public and private sectors, trading with a country known as Dilmun. Dilmun at this period was the name given to the island of Bahrain and perhaps to the part of the Eastern province of Saudi Arabia closest to it. The temple of Nannar also seems to have been actively involved in the trade, sometimes on its own account and sometimes as an investor in private enterprises.

What made Dilmun an important trading partner was that it acted as an entrepôt for copper, tin and other exotic goods coming up the Gulf from the mouth of the Indus as well as from modern south-west Iran. Mesopotamia, as we know, had to import all the metals that it required, so this trade was of vital importance to its economic survival. More glamorous goods like ivory, carnelian and lapis lazuli, together with exotic creatures like peacocks, also arrived from the south in small quantities, but copper was the core of the trade. It was shipped as ingots shaped like buns and these could be of variable quality. Ea-Nasir got into serious trouble with some of his customers for supplying them with substandard goods – ingots with too much of the waste products left in them! His business plainly had its ups and downs, and it seems that this is reflected in the changing fortunes of his house.

Initially, his house, 1 Old Street, was a large and commodious building with a chapel holding the family graves, a reception room and a generous number of other rooms. Then something seems to have gone wrong. Perhaps Ea-Nasir's financial situation deteriorated, or the old man died and the house had to be split up between the surviving children, as the law required. This seems to have made it necessary to wall off part of the building to the east of the court. These rooms then became part of the house at 7 Church Lane. The original house, now much smaller, developed a second entrance from the kitchen into an alley leading to Church Lane. A curious feature of this truncated house is that the former guest room, room 5, seems to have become a second chapel with another tomb in it. Does this suggest that a different family moved in?

Ea-Nasir was not alone in travelling to Dilmun; there was a group of merchants known collectively as the *alik Tilmun*, or those who go to Dilmun, and Ur was their home port. The trade does not seem to have been of major importance during the Ur III period, but it blossomed under the rulers of Isin and Larsa, perhaps because the kings of these dynasties were not powerful enough to control the trade down the Euphrates, an alternative route down which copper and timber could travel from Anatolia. There may even have been merchants from Dilmun living at Ur during the Isin-Larsa phase. One merchant mentioned in the texts had a name that incorporated the name of Dilmun's main god, Inzac, as one of its elements, suggesting that the man was probably of Dilmun origin.

Woolley excavated a curious little row of houses to the south-east of the ziggurat, in an area known as the EH site, on a terrace between the presumed line of the wall built by Ur-Nammu and the later Neo-Babylonian one (Fig. 8. iiia). The houses are quite unlike any of the others at Ur: they form a terrace of seven small dwellings, each with a courtyard and one or two small rooms at the rear. The entrance is placed so that it is not possible to see into the rooms. The back walls of the buildings form a straight line, while the front walls are stepped back. The closest parallels for this type of terraced house come from the contemporaneous site of Saar on the island of Bahrain, the heart of Dilmun (Fig. 8. iiib). There are differences as well: the Saar houses have washing and cooking facilities in standard positions, and these are not found at Ur, but the area was horribly disturbed. The Ur buildings are rather smaller and are associated with large numbers of tablets, said to be temple records. They also have graves beneath the floors, something not found at Saar.

It is interesting to speculate that there may have been a group of Dilmun merchants resident at Ur, perhaps under the protection of the temple, organizing the purchase of Mesopotamian goods in exchange for their metals. A small number of Dilmun seals, also found at Ur, could have been used for just this sort of transaction. These seals are stamp seals, by contrast with the cylinder seals of the local people, and the iconography is very distinctive. It must be stressed that the EH area was very disturbed and Woolley changed his mind about the nature of this terrace of buildings, originally thinking they may have been small funerary chapels, so any conclusions we draw are extremely speculative.

Chemical analysis can now detect the origin of much of the imported copper, but it is much more difficult to identify the goods going to Dilmun in exchange for the metals. Most of them seem to have been perishables, which, by their nature, leave little trace in the archaeological record. The texts give us some answers, but it is still unclear whether or not grain played a major part in the trade. It seems likely that it was not a major export as it is such a bulky commodity and of relatively low value. The texts speak of textiles of various sorts, some presumably highly fashionable and others more mundane, as well as leather goods like sandals, and sheepskin bags. We know that a gift of oil from Mari was sent to the 'king' of Dilmun. Scented oils were also produced in south Mesopotamia, so they, together with other luxuries like wine, may also have played a part in the trade.

Dilmun was not Ur's only trading partner at this time: merely the best-documented. Goods were also coming into the city from the north and east, as taxes as well as trade, but Mari could cut off the copper and timber coming down the Euphrates route if it was so minded, and routes over the Zagros Mountains from Iran were also liable to disruption by various petty kings and nomadic groups. The Gulf route seems to have been the most reliable. The Ur III state had an extremely efficient collection and redistribution system to gather taxes in kind and disburse the produce thus amassed from highly specialized industrial centres like the one at Puzrish Dagan, where large herds of livestock were gathered. These contributions were received as part of the *bala* system of taxation, levied on the core of the kingdom, and could then be sent out to temples and other institutions to supply their needs. The central bureaucracy set up by Ur-Nammu and Shulgi kept meticulous records of taxes owed and paid, and of amounts disbursed, using a simplified writing system and a reorganized system of weights and measures that had been introduced by these two kings. A number of scribal schools were set up to supply the next generation of 'civil servants'. These activities can all be identified in the huge number of tablets found at Ur.

The core area of the Ur III state was administered directly by the palace through this very large civil service, but the provinces were ruled jointly by a local governor, who was often a member of the local elite, and a military chief appointed by the king. The provinces were expected to contribute a special tax known as the *Gun mada* tax. This was paid by the military personnel stationed in each province on a sliding scale depending on rank. The top military man was usually in charge of collecting the tax, which seems to have been paid in livestock, and of delivering it to one or other of the central collection points. Other taxes in other commodities were also payable. In return for their livestock the provinces could receive grain and other commodities not available locally.

A centralized legal system was developed, with local law courts, and what might be called a court of appeal: the king in person. The earliest law code we know of is attributed to Ur-Nammu, or to Shulgi, and it is interesting to note that the penalties imposed are mostly financial. It is only under Hammurabi of Babylon that the principle of an eye for an eye, made famous by the Old Testament, is found. However, these early codes do not, in fact, lay down universally applicable laws, but seem to be the records of exceptional cases, possibly those tried by the king himself. They also start with a recital of the good deeds that the king has performed, such as the remission of debts, and some even lay down approved prices and rates of pay. It is not entirely unfair to say that they were, at least in part, propaganda documents intended to be read by the gods as much as the inhabitants of the city or kingdom, most of whom were illiterate. These tablets were stored in the *Edublalmah*, where justice was dispensed, as described in the last chapter.

We have already seen how the Ur III Dynasty collapsed, and how the centre of the city was brutally destroyed by the invading Elamites at the head of a coalition of foreigners. The Isin-Larsa kings who succeeded after the destruction were energetic in their rebuilding of the public buildings and the city flourished under their rule. It was the main port of entry for the valuable metal trade coming up the Gulf from as far away as the Indus valley, and became extremely

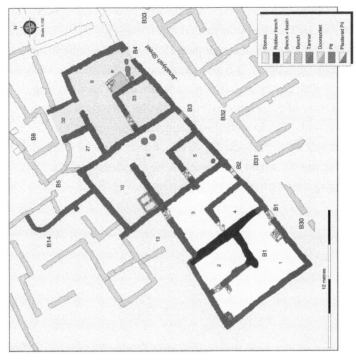

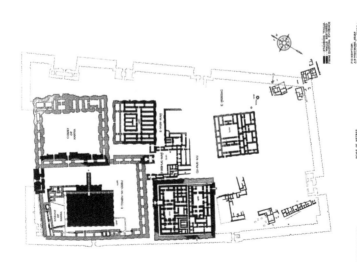

8.iiia and b Part of plan of EH site © British Museum and of Saar houses © R. Killick

prosperous. This wealth was reflected in the expansion of the domestic quarters of the city, as well as the reconstruction of many of the public buildings. However, the last king of Larsa, the powerful Rim-Sin, was finally overthrown by Hammurabi of Babylon. It is not clear how far this affected Ur. The major destruction visible in the archaeological levels seems to have taken place in the eleventh year of Samsu-iluna (his son), who records that in this year he destroyed the walls of Ur in retaliation against a revolt against him. It is probably to this event that we should date the destruction of many of the houses by fire. To ensure that the city would not rise again, he also destroyed much of the canal system, turning the south into a virtual desert.

Post-imperial Ur: Kassites to Neo-Babylonians

In the thirty-first year of his reign, Hammurabi of Babylon finally conquered his main rival, Rim-Sin, king of Larsa and overlord of Ur, thus bringing the south under his control. It is not clear how much devastation the city of Ur suffered, but Hammurabi set up a victory stela in the temenos (only fragments have been found). Two years later, he built a canal to bring water to Ur, and to a number of other southern cities. This seems to imply that the city was still inhabited and of some importance. However, there is no doubt about the destruction the city suffered after an ill-advised rebellion against Hammurabi's son Samsu-iluna, who destroyed the city walls and most of the major monuments, setting fire to the residential areas. He also apparently laid waste to the surrounding countryside, breaching the canals and destroying the agricultural base, thereby making living conditions almost impossible in the ruined city. In spite of this, some sort of life resumed, but the city did not really recover until after the fall of Hammurabi's dynasty, brought about by the raid on Babylon in c. 1595 BC by the Hittite king Mursilis. The raid seems to have resulted in the statue of Marduk, patron god of Babylon and its kings, being captured and carried away by the enemy – the final humiliation for the Hammurabi dynasty.

Little is known of the fate of Ur for the next 100 years or so. Two new dynasties are recorded in the texts: the kings of the Sealand Dynasty in the south, and the Kassite kings in the north. There is little textual evidence that can be attributed to either dynasty and, as a result, their history is poorly understood. The Kassites seem to have ruled for about 400, generally speaking, peaceful years from their new capital at Dur Kurigalsu (Aqar Quf), close to Baghdad. It is not known for certain where they came from, but it is generally thought that their homeland was probably in the Zagros Mountains to the north and east of Assyria. Occasional references are found to them as soldiers and farm labourers from about the 1770s BC onwards, by which time they seem to have reached the middle Euphrates.

By around 1400 BC, the Kassite kings of Babylonia were firmly established and were major players on the world stage, exchanging brotherly greetings with the Egyptian and Hittite kings and consolidating these diplomatic ties with royal marriages. All these manoeuvres can be followed in the famous Amarna archives from Egypt, written in cuneiform on clay tablets, and found at Amarna itself. The rulers also exchanged valuable 'presents', although the value of the gifts had to be carefully balanced so that the worth was the same in each direction. The Kassite king complained rather petulantly if he felt he was not receiving a fair return for his investment! The Kassites received quantities of gold from Egypt and were able to supply precious lapis lazuli, chariots and horses in exchange. Some of this lapis may have arrived by sea via the Persian Gulf and the Kassites safeguarded this valuable trade route by putting a Kassite governor in charge of the islands of Bahrain, again an important entrepôt.

It was a Kassite king called Kurigalsu, who probably came to the throne some time in the second half of the fourteenth century BC, who set about refurbishing the city of Ur, returning it to something like its former glory. Kurigalsu proved to be a very energetic restorer of temples, but introduced few new ideas, perhaps either because the Kassites had no tradition of monumental mud-brick building in their homeland, or because he did not wish to outrage local susceptibilities by departing from tradition. One Kassite innovation made a lasting impression: it was a new way of decorating the façades of buildings. Some now showed huge figures in high relief made of specially moulded bricks. The best example can be seen on the façade of the Karaindash temple at Uruk, the walls of which are covered with niches containing standing figures of gods and goddesses, their hands clasped round vases, and separated from each other by flowing water (Fig. 9.i). Sadly, at Ur, we only have a few broken pieces of moulded bricks to suggest that such decoration might have been used here too.

Kurigalsu's efforts were focused on the temenos area. We do not know with certainty if he worked on the ziggurat itself, because major works in the Neo-Babylonian period swept away all the previous modifications later than the Third dynasty. His inscriptions claim that he did and there is no reason to doubt them. He certainly rebuilt the wall of the temenos and the temple of Ningal, wife of the moon god Nanna, which stood close to the southern corner of the ziggurat enclosure. His building apparently followed the plan of earlier shrines, but the walls are thin and rather shoddily built. In an innovation, a gateway in the south-east wall of the great courtyard in front of the Ningal shrine now

9.i Figure from the Kassite temple at Uruk by Tessa Rickards

gave direct access to the restored *Gigparku*, home of the high priestess. This was enlarged, and seems to have been almost entirely residential. In its southern half, the great Ningal temple characterizes the earlier buildings, but has disappeared. Perhaps this is because the building was now directly linked to the Ningal temple in the ziggurat enclosure and another shrine might have been thought redundant.

Some of Kurigalsu's most successful and impressive work can be seen in the expanded and restored temple of the *Edublalmah,* some of which still survives today. This building had acted as a place of judgement and a library where decisions on the cases could be stored in both the Ur III and Isin-Larsa periods. Kurigalsu found the earlier buildings in a bad state, so he cut down the standing walls evenly and then piously enclosed them in a platform on which his new building was erected. The outside of the building was decorated with T-shaped grooves, and, due to the new platform (also decorated with the grooves), had to be approached by a flight of steps. It consisted of two chambers, one behind the other, and the walls of the back room were so thick that Woolley suggested it had originally been domed. Remarkably, the arched doorways to the inner and outer rooms were still intact when first uncovered by J. E. Taylor in 1885, and one was still standing when re-excavated by Woolley. It survives to this day.

The *Edublalmah* opened on to a large courtyard to the south-east. It was approached from the east by a sort of sacred way, controlled by three gates separated by courts. This passage also gave access to a new temple, squeezed between the east wall of the *Edublalmah* and the west wall of the rebuilt *Enunmah*, or treasury, whose plan was almost unchanged. The restoration and expansion of the *Edublalmah* strongly suggests that Ur remained an important centre in the administration of justice, even under a new and probably foreign dynasty. To the west of the court was another gate giving access to the *Gigparku*, as described above. There was also a second flight of stairs giving direct access to the ziggurat terrace. To the south of the courtyard there were what may have been workshops, and a number of magazines for storage.

Beyond the sacred precinct was the lower town, now also surrounded by a thick rampart that was sufficiently wide to allow buildings on top of it. The backs of these buildings served as a further barrier to an attacker, as seen in the previous chapter. There is a new feature on the north-east stretch of the city wall, where a large square salient carries a two-roomed structure with immensely thick walls, built in typical Kassite fashion with an inner and an outer face of fine baked brick. The space between them was filled with rubble. The building is not a temple; its position and the very strong walls suggest it was a fort, standing above the canal to flank the town on this side. Adjacent to it, and protected by it, are traces of a passage through the rampart leading to what Woolley suggested might have been a water gate. Such a gate would have been essential, especially in times of siege, for resupplying the town with food and water. On the south-east wall are the remains of a temple dedicated to Ningizzida or Nin-Ezen, one of the Underworld gods, so we can say that the ramparts were defended both by man and the supernatural power of the gods. The temple was rebuilt and enlarged by Kurigalsu, but is badly damaged and the plan is unclear. A later Kassite rebuild was less badly damaged, and seems to have been on a different plan. There are no inscribed bricks, so we do not know the identity of the builder of this later temple.

Only rather fragmentary remains of Kassite private houses were found – some, as we have seen, on the city wall, and more in the AH site above the earlier Ur III/Isin-Larsa/Old Babylonian houses (see previous chapter). The traditional courtyard house still seems to be the norm, but there is no sign of the chapels found in the richer Larsa houses, though a few burials still occur below the floors. Some are similar in construction to the older ones with a brick-vaulted grave, but some are simply two pots laid on the ground mouth-to-mouth, with the body crammed inside. The graves are mostly rather poorly furnished with a little jewellery, some pots and sometimes a seal. This relative poverty may reflect the decline in importance of the city, which remained a religious centre but seems to have lost its commercial and administrative primacy. Only a few small finds can be definitely dated to the Kassite period, the most common being more of the familiar terracotta figurines made in a mould. Some of the designs show humans, some protective deities and some animals. One example shows an elephant, a reminder that the Syrian elephant was not hunted to extinction until the last century of the first millennium BC, so we do not have to presume that it was an exotic import (Fig. 9.iib). (Some scholars would actually date these figures back to the Isin-Larsa period.) Generally speaking, the levels belonging to the period are rather disturbed, making it very difficult to date small finds or even pottery forms to a specific period.

One artefact type of undoubted Kassite date, and an innovation of the period, are the splendid *Kudurrus* or boundary stones. They are usually of hard stone, often black or dark greenish, and carry the details of land grants made by the king. They are decorated with rows of miniature altars, or perhaps temple façades, each topped with the symbol of one of the great gods. They seem to have been erected to commemorate gifts of land by the king to his followers,

9.ii a and b Moulded terraotta figures: a human couple and an elephant by Mary Shepperson

and to record the conditions on which the grant was made. We do not know if they were erected on the boundaries of the land itself, or were kept in a temple where the contract could be preserved for all time.

The later fourteenth century saw the re-emergence of Assyria as an important power in north Mesopotamia, leading to rising tension between Assyria and the Kassites. Eventually, a diplomatic marriage sealed an uneasy pact, but shortly afterwards the young son of this marriage was deposed from the Babylonian throne by a usurper and killed. The Assyrian king Ashur-uballit, incensed by the murder of his grandson, stormed down to Babylonia, killed the usurper and installed a new Kassite king. The Assyrian influence did not last long, and the names of fifteen or sixteen more Kassite kings are known, though their importance was hugely diminished and their kingdom truncated. It seems that the Sealand Dynasty – people based in the very south of the country who were also known as Chaldeans – may have taken control of Ur at some point and this is probably when Ur earned the designation 'Ur of the Chaldees'.

The political focus shifts emphatically northwards to the kingdom of Assyria with the successors of Ashur-uballit and the so-called Middle Assyrian period, from the mid-fourteenth century to the late eleventh. It seems that for several centuries Ur crumbled in peace. Not only was its political influence at an end, but as the head of the Persian Gulf had retreated southwards its function as a vital port for trade in metals coming up the Gulf also ended. The Gulf route had become less important for other reasons, too, because the Assyrians now controlled traffic along the Euphrates and the Tigris, down which metals could travel from the Anatolian Highlands: a shorter and easier route. A lucrative overland metal-trade route from Aššur to central Anatolia is chronicled in the unique cuneiform documents from Kultepe/Kanesh. These tell us that Assyrian merchants took textiles by donkey caravan from Aššur to Kultepe where they were exchanged, via a network of smaller market towns, for precious metals. These were then taken back to Aššur on the backs of the merchants. The trade was funded by investors from both the private and the state sectors, who put up money. This went into a so-called sack, or kitty, and the profits were shared out in proportion to the 'investment' on the return home.

By the early first millennium BC, our sources are dramatically improved and it is possible to trace the rise of the Assyrian empire. This is one of the best-known periods of Mesopotamian history today, thanks in large part to the excavations of Henry Layard at Nineveh and other major cities in the north. He brought home with him the wonderful palace reliefs portraying major episodes in the empire's history laid out like a strip cartoon. These, and human-headed bulls, guarded the palaces of the rulers, and can now be seen in the British Museum in London. The centre of power had shifted decisively to the north, but Assyrian control extended to the head of the Gulf as well. A new chapter in Ur's history came in the seventh century with the appointment by the Assyrians of a very active and pious governor of the city, Sinbalatsu-iqbi, who succeeded his father to the job. The archaeological evidence shows that he found the sacred buildings in a parlous state. The courtyard of the *Edublalmah*, built by the Kassite kings, had filled up completely with rubble, so that the shrine itself no longer stood on a plinth but was at ground level. Instead of digging out the courtyard, the governor laid a new floor over the rubbish and decided to add an extra room to each side of the shrine, thus expanding the building to fill one side of the new court completely. He built with rather crumbly bricks, which are easily recognizable even when no building inscriptions were found, and the workmanship was poor. The new rooms were incorporated into the façade of the temple by means of a thick coat of plaster covering both old and new walls, which was then whitewashed. The governor boasted of the great door he had erected in the shrine, made of boxwood and decorated with precious metals. No trace of this survives today, but its extant door pivot was a reutilized Kassite *kudurru* or boundary marker.

Sinbalatsu-iqbi also did major work on the temenos wall, with a new revetment shoring up the older walls, and rebuilt above the ruined *Gigparku*. The new building was on a different plan from the old and very little of it remains. However, below its pavements were found groups of protective, mould-made figurines covered in a lime wash with details painted on, usually in black. The custom of burying such figurines seems to have been imported from Assyria and some of them are very reminiscent of the protective deities seen on the Assyrian wall reliefs. There is a bird-headed winged figure and another which seems to be wearing a fish-skin, both to be found on the reliefs. There are also human figures with animal heads, and a collection of dogs, some standing and some squatting. The figures are found both singly and in groups, close to the walls of the rooms. In the case of the ones belonging to Sin-Balatsu-iqbi's building, they stood in what Woolley described as sentry boxes (made of three plano-convex bricks), and were accompanied by little offerings of grain and small birds. Plano-convex bricks had not been in use for more than a millennium, so either they were specially made for the purpose or they were disinterred from the ruins of older buildings, suggesting that they were considered to have special powers themselves.

After the death of Ashurbanipal, the Assyrian Empire began to fall apart, leaving a vacuum on the political scene, which was quickly filled by a new dynasty with its seat at Babylon. Two of its kings were especially important in the history of Ur: Nebuchadnezzar and Nabonidus. The latter had a special devotion to the moon god, apparently because he had been born at Harran, another centre for the worship of Nannar/Sin. His mother may even have been a priestess at the main temple there. Given this background, it is unsurprising that Ur once again became an important place of worship for the moon god, Nannar, and that massive building works were carried out there, especially by Nabonidus. The amount of building works undertaken at Ur is a barometer of the importance of the site on the political or religious scene at any one time. The works may also have had a second purpose as an attempt by the new dynasty to placate and win over the conservative priesthood to support their new masters and establish legitimacy.

The remains of the Neo-Babylonian period have suffered badly from erosion and, to a lesser degree, from the mining of the site for precious baked bricks to be reused elsewhere for new buildings. In spite of this, Woolley was able to recover the plan of the sacred area in some detail and to recreate a picture of its former magnificence. Some of his reconstructions, notably the one of the ziggurat itself, should perhaps be treated with a little scepticism.

Nebuchadnezzar of Babylon, the second ruler of the dynasty, seems to have rebuilt and enlarged the temenos wall. This had largely been silted up, so that there was little separation between the sacred areas and the rest of the city. The new wall was a magnificent structure enclosing a larger area than ever before, rectangular, and formed of two parallel walls, each 3.5 metres thick, with intra-mural rooms between them, giving a total thickness of about 11 metres. There are some slight changes in direction within the wall, which Woolley attributed to the individual stretches having been built by different gangs of workers. It must have been a tense moment when two gangs met up! The outer stretches of the walls were decorated with the usual buttressing and recessing suitable for religious buildings and, in the west, two stairs gave access to the roof of the wall where troops could be deployed if necessary. As in earlier periods, the wall may have functioned as a last redoubt in the event of attack. It was further strengthened by what seem to be two forts, one in the west corner and the second in the south. The three great gates on the east side were heavily defended with pylons and guard chambers, as was the one on the south-east wall.

The most northerly of these gates, the Nannar gate, led to the Nannar court, which in turn gave on to the ziggurat terrace. The pavement of the court had silted up over the years and, rather than clear it out, Nebuchadnezzar filled it in and re-floored it to be level with the upper terrace. The middle gate, known as the Bursin gate because of the inscribed bricks found in it, was connected by a great drain that ran up to a flight of steps giving access to the ziggurat terrace. The third, or Cyrus, gate had been much patched and modified, but curiously did not have a guard chamber. It may originally have given access to the remains of the old Kassite sacred way (see p. 124). The two entrances on the second long side of the enclosure were apparently more in the way of service gates and were not well preserved.

The whole temenos area was dominated by the great ziggurat, as it had been since the third millennium. Nebuchadnezzar had apparently done some work here, but it was Nabonidus who was responsible for a major redesign. Any work done by Nebuchadnezzar was apparently cleared away by Nabonidus, as not a single brick of his was found in the ziggurat. According to his own inscriptions, Nabonidus was a stickler for precedent, and must have disliked the repairs done by his predecessor, perhaps because he thought them uncanonical. The lowest stage on Ur-Nammu's ziggurat was used as the base for Nabonidus's new works, as were the three stairways giving access to the top of it, which was levelled off. The ground in front of the stairs had risen by about a metre, so it was necessary to raise the level of the lowest stairs too, and to repair them. No trace of the gatehouse at first-floor level survives, but the pylons supporting the Ur-Nammu structures were so solid that Woolley suggests they were reused by Nabonidus. Above this, few remains allow for a definitive reconstruction. All that was found above this level were the remains of a single small stair at the north end of the terrace, which presumably gave access to the second stage, and the remains of the casing wall of the second stage. Originally, it was thought that there had been a spiral stair going up to the shrine on the topmost level. This idea was discarded as structurally unlikely, and small stairs, like the one found, were suggested at the north end of the first stage and at the south end on the next stage, and so on, giving almost the illusion of a spiral stair.

The number of stages is unknown, but the presence of so much rubble, which had eroded down from the upper part of the ziggurat, led to Woolley suggesting that there might originally have been seven of them rising to an estimated height of 160 feet. However, he also said that 'if the height [required to achieve seven stages] be still thought excessive it could be cut down by two stages without loss of symmetry'. He had apparently been influenced by discussions with the German archaeologist Walter Andrae, who had excavated at Babylon itself. This number of stages was suggested for the ziggurat at Babylon largely because of the famous description by Herodotus. Herodotus also describes the small shrine on top of the ziggurat there, with its golden furniture, where a priestess slept alone, awaiting the arrival of the god. It is difficult to know how much credence to give Herodotus, owing to his aforementioned fondness for a good story. The Babylonian ziggurat was also said to have been multicoloured to represent the different parts of the cosmos, and Woolley showed that the lowest stage of the Ur ziggurat was certainly painted black, while the shrine and perhaps the top stage had been faced with blue-glazed bricks, of which large numbers were found lying in the rubble. There is slight evidence for an intermediate stage being painted white, while another may have been red. The black at the base would have represented the Underworld, the red the earth, the blue the sky and a postulated gold dome on the shrine would have represented heaven.

The ziggurat was built with layers of reeds and matting between the mud-brick courses, and Taylor even found evidence for some timber lacing. The timber was said to be teak. Such lacing may have been intended to give the structure some movement in the event of earthquakes: it is a technique widely seen in Turkey today. Above a certain level, Woolley reports that the mud bricks were red and suggested that the colour was the result of the damp reeds catching fire and smouldering for long periods, thus lightly firing the bricks in a reducing atmosphere. The whole structure was enclosed in mud plaster. Nabonidus contrived to find the foundation inscriptions of some of the Third Dynasty builders, which he quoted on his own foundation cylinders that were placed one in each corner of the ziggurat. Taylor was able to find all four of them (see chapter 1).

Two new structures appear in this period: the first in the angle between the north pier supporting the main stair and the lateral stair against the north-west façade of the ziggurat terrace, and the second on the other side of the main stair between the southern pier and the lateral stair on the south-east façade. The first is thought to have been a shrine to Nannar, what the Germans called a *Tieftempel*, to balance the *Hochtempel* on the top of the ziggurat. The other was called the Boat shrine by Woolley, but its function is unknown. Both buildings had suffered badly from erosion, and the Nannar shrine seems to have been deliberately cut down before thin Persian walls were built over it. The entrance to the temple courtyard on the north-east side is carefully aligned with the entrance to the great Nannar courtyard. This, in turn, was aligned with the Nannar gate in the temenos wall. Beyond this court (or room) are four more rooms, of which the one against the ziggurat has a raised pavement, but none of the fixtures one might expect in a temple can be seen. The so-called Boat shrine does not extend to the façade of the ziggurat and there is a 'dead' space between the two. The area was particularly badly eroded. The building is entered from the north-west and the large court or room has two narrow rooms along its north-west side, which probably supported a stair. The court gives access to a rectangular room paved with burnt brick, which is almost entirely filled with a rectangular burnt-brick support or platform. Woolley describes it as 'a support of burnt brick standing five courses high and narrowing at the northwest end'. His epigraphist, Dr Legrain, suggested that the platform had originally supported a model of the boat in which Nannar crossed the sky. The room contained a large amount of wood ash, which might possibly lend some support to this idea, though it seems to derive largely from classical mythology.

To the south of the ziggurat the Assyrian governor had rebuilt a temple to Ningal, the wife of the moon god Nannar, following the precedent set by the Kassite king Kurigalsu. Nabonidus in his turn set about restoring Sinbalatsu-iqbi's temple and embellishing it further. He changed little except to run a double wall to link its north corner to the corner of the ziggurat. The temple was not well preserved, and in some places the walls could only be reconstructed by tracing the edges of the burnt brick pavements, which survived better. The sanctuary was raised above the level of the other rooms and so was approached by a flight of steps. It had a curious screen wall in it, built to form three sides of a square, and it is thought that the walls enclosed and protected the statue of the goddess. It is possible that it was further protected by a curtain that formed the fourth side. Apart from this, the other remarkable feature of this temple is its huge recessed pylons on either side of the entrance to the antechamber, which, in turn, gave access to the shrine itself. Finally, in this corner of the terrace, lying between the temple and the temenos wall, was another building entered by a triple gate built with very heavy walls, the function of which is unclear. Perhaps it is a rebuilding of the fort that stood in this position a little earlier and is thought to have given access to the top of the temenos wall? The thickness of the walls would seem to support this.

Moving down from the ziggurat terrace, but still within the wider temenos, we see to the south-east of the ziggurat the remains of what were originally three separate buildings: the *Enunmah*, the *Edublalmah* and the *Gigparku* (some of the oldest buildings apart from the ziggurat itself). As in the previous period, the latter two were combined into a single unit, and the *Gigparku* seems to have been composed of a number of different domestic and work areas, having lost its temple and the formal living quarters of the priestess. Although an inscription of Nabonidus says that he 'built for Sin the house of the *entu*', his daughter, Bel-Shalti-Nannar, who filled the role of high priestess, had another bigger and better palace near the north harbour (Fig. 9.iii). The *Edublalmah* was left as it had been after the work carried out by Sinbalatsu-iqbi, but was refurbished by Nebuchadnezzar, who laid a new pavement in the courtyard in front of the shrine, while Nabonidus laid another. There also seems to have been a subsidiary shrine in the western annex. The continuity in plan suggests that its function as a law court continued as before.

The remains of school tablets and syllabaries, one of which is inscribed 'Property of the boys' school', as well as abacuses, suggest that the rooms on the west side of the court between the *Edublalmah* and the *Giparu* may have been used for a boys' school no doubt to train up the priesthood of the future.

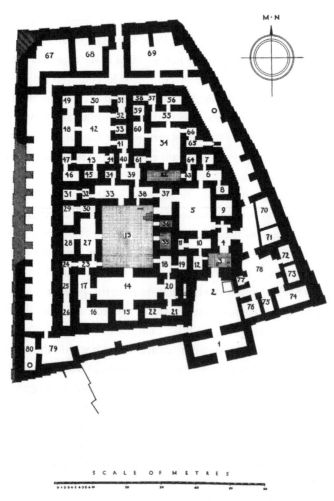

9.iii Palace of Bel-Shalti-Nannar © British Museum

Under two of the rooms were found foundation deposits of rather charming copper models of dogs, which were supposed to protect the inhabitants from harm. The boys were also provided with a 'museum', perhaps to demonstrate how the script had evolved and to prove its sacred antiquity. The objects included tablets of Ur III date, an inscribed foundation cone from the Kassite period and part of a statue of Shulgi in diorite with the inscription carefully preserved. There was also a Kassite *kudurru* and various pots and jars of clay. It seems that Nabonidus's daughter was as interested in the past as he was.

The gate on the north-west side of the great court led into a maze of rooms, which gave access to the *Enunmah* originally built as a treasury in the Ur III period. Its central block of five rooms remained unchanged from the previous period, with shrines to Ningal and Nannar in the two central rooms, but Nebuchadnezzar opened up what had been some of the best-hidden and most secure rooms on the temenos. He laid down a large courtyard in front of the antechamber to the shrines and built two ranges of rooms one on each side of the court. The third part of the court, the most southerly and the lowest, extended south, over the old Kassite sacred way.

Under the pavement of Nebuchadnezzar, in the west corner of room 5 of the Ningal shrine, a remarkable collection of artefacts was found. It included objects of gold, silver and bronze. Among these were a pin with a standing female figure on the head covered in gold leaf, two solid gold bracelets and a fine collection of gold brooches, rings, earrings, some decorated with delicate filigree work and beads of semi-precious stones. There was also a silver jug and two bronze bowls, one of which contained some cylindrical silver goblets. The jewellery seems to be of several different dates, with some pieces, such as the etched carnelian beads, dating back to the third millennium. An ivory box lid, bearing a Phoenician inscription dedicating the object to Astarte, was also found, which may originally have held some of the smaller items of the treasure.

From the same room came two ivory combs, one with a splendid engraving of a bull, ivory handles and an ivory palette in the shape of a sphinx. Other ivory objects included a spoon with the handle formed of two cheerful, squat human figures, found below Nebuchadnezzar's pavement in the courtyard, and a circular ivory box decorated with a procession of slightly Egyptian-looking human figures. It seems likely that the objects were temple offerings made over the millennia and hidden for safety when the city came under attack from the Persian army. The variety of the gifts underlines the range of overseas contacts under the Neo-Babylonian 'emperors' and the wealth of the donors.

Religious buildings were not confined to the temenos. The Nin-ezen temple on the city wall was rebuilt and the new plan partly overlaid the previous temples built by Larsa and Kassite kings. Once again great ingenuity was used to trace its plan, as the walls were very badly denuded. A line of white, the remnants of the wall plaster which had trickled down between the wall face and the floors, could be traced to give the outline of the plan. It was probably built by the indefatigable Sinbalatsu-iqbi and then refurbished by Nebuchadnezzar, whose stamped bricks were found in the forecourt. Another impressive, but anonymous, temple was excavated by the north harbour. It was a solid rectangular building which measured 33 metres by 37 metres, the walls of which were faced with burnt brick. What makes it remarkable is that what survives is the substructure of the temple, which had been filled with clean sand. There is a long tradition in south Mesopotamian religious architecture, which goes back well into the third millennium BC, of building a mirror image below ground of the structure above. It seems that the substructure was as holy as the temple itself and was required to be ritually cleaned – hence the clean sand. The plan of this temple is rather different from the ones we are used to, with a third room behind the shrine and its forecourt. It is not known what it was used for, but Woolley, with his unerring eye for a good story, declared the third room to be an oracle chamber!

From the entry of this temple, which was at the west corner, a solid mass of mud brick, forming a sort of causeway, ran towards the splendid palace of Bel-Shalti-Nannar, the *entu* priestess and daughter of Nabonidus. His inscriptions refer to the building as the *Egigpar*, home of the *entu* priestess (Fig. 9. iii). The building is trapezoidal in shape and the whole structure slopes from the ramparts of the city in the north-east to towards the harbour in the south-east. The external walls were buttressed on three sides, but on the fourth or east side is a new feature: curious arrowhead buttresses, which form a pattern like the teeth of a saw. They are present on the internal wall. Once inside the main entrance, access was tightly controlled to the interior, which was formed of four separate units each based round a courtyard. Each courtyard gave access to a large reception room and a series of smaller ones. The whole structure was insulated from the outer wall by a passage running all round the building, which was probably vaulted to judge from the remains of buttressing on both sides, and in the south-east corner was a self-contained unit, which might have been for the commander of the guard. A much smaller gate was found on the north wall; this may have been a sort of servants' entrance, with storage rooms on either side. This building is said to be similar to structures found at Babylon.

Few private houses of the Neo-Babylonian period were excavated, but a limited area (NH) was dug close to the area of Larsa houses described in Chapter 8. From this small exposure, it looks as if the layout of the buildings was more regular than it had been in earlier towns, suggesting a degree of town planning. There is a wide street separating two rows of houses, which meets another slightly smaller road at right angles, and an alley leading off what may be an open area. One house stands out because of its size and the fact that the external walls are decorated with the same saw-toothed pattern of buttresses that we saw on Nabonidus's *Gigparku*. It has forty rooms and two or possibly three courtyards. The size and external decoration suggest that it may have been something more than a private house. Rooms 22 and 23, which together probably comprised a courtyard, contained a large number of school tablets and syllabaries, and it looks as if this fairly self-contained suite of rooms may have been a school. Given the grandeur of the building, it is tempting to ask if it was set up to educate the children of senior officials. The other houses are smaller and continue to be built on the courtyard plan with a reception room, which has one or more smaller rooms opening off it. Two of the other houses also have stretches of external saw-tooth buttressing and several contain tablets, which seem to represent family archives.

Large numbers of graves were found close to the surface of the mound, many of them exposed by erosion and thoroughly looted. The few surviving bits and pieces were often difficult to date. They will all be discussed in the next chapter.

10

Death and Afterlife

In 539 BC, Cyrus conquered Babylon, ending the Neo-Babylonian Empire. His bricks are found at Ur and, as he died the year after his success, he must have begun the work here very soon after the fall of Babylon. We find his bricks in the most southerly of the great gates into the temenos, for instance, which Woolley called the Cyrus gate. He mended the temenos wall and refurbished the *Enunmah*, taking down the additional wings added by Nebuchadnezzar, but leaving the core of five rooms that had existed for almost two thousand years. It is possible that the work was completed by Cyrus's successor, Cambyses, using up the bricks already made for Cyrus's programme of restoration. Cyrus's attentions were not all constructive, and it seems that the ziggurat itself was thoroughly desecrated and that flimsy workshops, kilns and houses were built over the north-western part of the ziggurat terrace. It is difficult to know what else the Persian rulers may have done, because erosion has destroyed so much of the top of the mounds.

Erosion has also destroyed the upper levels in much of the town, but many tablets of the Persian period survive and indicate that the town regained its prosperity under the Persian overlords. The tablets found most recently date even later, to the twelfth year of Alexander. There are also many graves exposed on the surface, which have been thoroughly robbed. In a few instances where preservation is better, as in the NH area described in the previous chapter, graves are found under the floors of the fragmentary remains of houses. It is very difficult to date the empty graves, as some of the methods of burial are common to both the Neo-Babylonian and Persian periods. However, the brick vault under a house floor, seen first in the houses of Ur III date, becomes increasingly uncommon and by the Neo-Babylonian period has virtually disappeared. The clay coffins with one straight end and one rounded one, on the other hand, are found exclusively in the upper levels. In two burials, the clay coffin held an inner one made of copper, held together by copper stays. It was only when they had been sent for cleaning that charming decoration of animals and flowers on the stays was revealed (Fig. 10.i).

The end for Ur seems to have come when the Euphrates River shifted its course eastwards, leaving the city without water. The shift seems to have come gradually, as two Persian burials were found in the bed of the great canal that ran around the eastern side of Ur, indicating that the city was still struggling on even after the canal dried up. One can imagine the gradual depopulation as water became scarcer and scarcer and agricultural productivity ceased. Where the people went we do not know, but in fact the desiccation turned out to be a blessing in disguise – at least for the archaeologists – as it left the empty city stranded in a sandy waste, unvisited except by the Bedu for more than 1,500 years. It was only in the nineteenth century that foreigners began to explore the area again (see Chapter 1).

From 1922, when Woolley began his excavations, Ur was in a sense reborn as its history was uncovered and tourists began to visit the site once more. Its fame spread with the publication by Woolley of lavish photographs of his most

10.i Decoration on Persian coffin stay by Mary Shepperson

sensational finds in the popular magazine *The Illustrated News*. Then, as noted in Chapter 1, Agatha Christie published her *Murder in Mesopotamia*, which was widely believed to be based on her visits to Ur, first as the guest of Woolley and then later as the wife of Max Mallowan, who was the longest-serving of Woolley's assistants. All this publicity increased public interest, which was further boosted when some of the magnificent finds were displayed in the British Museum. No further archaeological work was carried out at Ur by the British Museum after Woolley's last season in 1934, although he continued to work on the publications until his death. Some restoration work was carried out later by Iraqi archaeologists.

The site next came to public attention in a much less agreeable way. The human tragedy of the two Gulf Wars in 1991 and 2003 is well documented, as is the damage to Iraq's irreplaceable heritage. After the invasion of Kuwait by Saddam Hussein in 1990, punitive sanctions were imposed on Iraq and real poverty gripped small farmers and labourers, who were in some cases unable to feed their families. The failed uprising by the Shia of the south in the aftermath of the invasion of 1991 led to brutal repression by Saddam and to even greater hardship. The uprising also led to a rash of looting in thirteen provincial museums and the spoils were quickly smuggled out of the country and sold on, in some cases raising large sums of money. The possibility of making quick and relatively easy money with which to feed their families led many farmers to visit their local archaeological sites and to dig for anything saleable. As the Iraqi Antiquities service was being increasingly starved of funds by the government, there were few guards present to protect the sites; the looting began in earnest between the two Gulf Wars and continued unabated for fifteen years or more. Looting became a business, and gangs of looters armed with guns as well as shovels would chase off any guards there were, descend on a site and rip the guts out of it.

The most high-profile looting of the second Gulf War was that of the National Museum in Baghdad in 2003. In spite of repeated requests to the Ministry of Defence and the Pentagon to secure the museum before and during the invasion, the looting seems to have continued unchecked for three days, leaving behind a scene of devastation. It is still not known exactly how many artefacts were stolen, as many of them were still waiting to be accessioned and so had not been added to the museum's inventory, but the total may have been as high as 15,000. In addition, offices were vandalized with doors stoved in, papers ripped from cabinets, card indices thrown to the floor and everything movable taken. The wall that disguised the entrance to a secure storeroom was breached, and many items stolen, including a high proportion of the cylinder seals stored there. Fortunately, many of the most valuable items, including most of the objects from the royal graves at Ur, had been moved to the vaults of the National Bank before the invasion. Even there they were not safe, and because of serious damage to the water system they were flooded by sewage that seeped into the vault and into the trunks in which they were stored. Some of the famous ivories from Nimrud are thought to have been damaged beyond repair.

The looting of the museum seems to have been carried out by different groups. One of them was knowledgeable and knew exactly what they wanted, possibly stealing to order. Another group was less particular and took any antiquities they could find, including replicas from the museum shop, while the third took everything they could lay their hands on, including office equipment and light fittings. A list of between forty and fifty of the most important missing antiquities was quickly compiled and efforts were focused on retrieving them. This task fell mainly to Colonel Matthew Bogdanos of the American Marines, who has written a very exciting account of his work (see further reading). It appears that between a third and a half of the objects stolen have now been recovered – some returned by Baghdadis who had taken them into their own homes for safekeeping after the looting, some tracked down by Bogdanos and some seized by customs officials across the world. No major finds from Ur were taken.

After the invasion, the allies became belatedly aware of the damage that had been done and began to plan for reparation. It must be remembered that Iraq had been under sanctions since the invasion of Kuwait in 1990 and this meant that almost all contacts with the outside world had been cut off. Books and journals could no longer be acquired and internet access was impossible. The academic community in Iraq was unable to keep in touch with its peers outside the country and no new ideas or equipment entered the country, leaving scholars, in many cases, twenty years behind the times. As a result, the need for training and even basic equipment was acute. Damage was not limited to the heritage section; libraries and universities were also ransacked and many priceless books and papers lost, while historic buildings such as the Malwiya minaret in Samarra were vandalized.

Various initiatives were taken by the allies to improve the situation. The Italians supplied and fitted a new conservation laboratory at the National Museum in Baghdad, and provided some basic training in conservation; the Italians, Poles and Germans began to train and equip a new corps of site guards to try to stop the looting of sites and UNESCO co-ordinated the efforts;

the Italian carabinieri began to build up a computerized database of objects in the National Museum, and to list objects known to have been stolen; the Americans, Germans and British also provided training, especially in conservation, heritage management and computing. The British Museum's plan to take a team of conservators to Baghdad to continue the training there had to be cancelled due to the deteriorating security situation. Some of these training initiatives continue, especially in Kurdistan, but the security situation still prevents large-scale efforts in the south. Many smaller organizations such as the British School of Archaeology in Iraq (now British Institute for the Study of Iraq) also attempted to help with books, equipment and training. Efforts were also made by a number of countries, notably Japan, to provide new equipment, which included new cases for the museums, new books for their libraries and computing equipment.

In 2005 and 2007, Dr John Curtis, then keeper of the Ancient Near East department at the British Museum, was able to carry out a detailed survey of the damage caused by the military at Babylon and a less complete survey of damage at Ur. The situation at Ur was less bad than that at Babylon, where enormous damage had been done. Sometime before 1991, an important military airbase called Tallil had been set up close to Ur by the Iraqi military. The roar of fighter planes taking off and the rumble of heavy trucks and machinery all shook the ancient buildings, which had already been damaged in some cases by inappropriate restoration using modern materials. More direct damage was caused to the ziggurat by an American air raid thought to have taken place in 1991 in response to anti-aircraft fire from the base that had hit an American warplane. The ziggurat is marked on the south-eastern façade with bullet, shell and shrapnel holes; further damage also occurred after the camp was taken over by the Americans, whose perimeter fence enclosed the whole of the archaeological site, which at least protected it from looting. On the other hand, some inappropriate construction went on within the base for car parks and auxiliary buildings.

The most serious damage inflicted by the Americans came when they built a large fortified entrance to the camp known as the Visitor Control Centre over the largely unexplored suburb of Ur called Diqdiqqa. This gate has now been dismantled in order to limit the damage. Additional problems were caused in 2008 when rockets fired by insurgents into the base fell close to the area of early second-millennium BC housing known as the AH site (see Chapter 8). The Americans finally withdrew from the base in 2011; it is now known as the Imam Ali base and is again used by the Iraqi military.

*

This book has tried to chart the fortunes of the city of Ur from its beginnings in the sixth millennium BC as a small village within the vast marshes at the head of the Persian Gulf, and to follow its development, first to a town at the centre of a small city state in the mid-third millennium and then, by the end of the millennium, to a city at the heart of the Ur III Empire. The city was laid waste by Samsu-iluna of Babylon around 1800 BC, but gradually came back to life under the Kassite kings as a provincial capital and religious centre – a position it seems to have retained under the Assyrian and then the Neo-Babylonian kings. One of these, Nabonidus, was especially devoted to the moon god Sin, patron of the city, and carried out massive building works. The Persian conquerors also seem to have acknowledged the special status of Ur, but the movement of the Euphrates eastwards into a new course removed its source of water and spelled the end of the city.

There is much still to be discovered and much work still to be done at Ur itself and in the immediate vicinity. We know little of the smaller settlements that are likely to have surrounded it. New work has recently begun at one such site close to Ur called Tell Khaiber, a special-purpose site with a large administrative building dating to the early years of the second millennium BC. This work is being carried out by a British expedition, while an aerial survey of the surroundings of the city is also being undertaken by an Italian team. New research will soon be possible online thanks to an ambitious project between the British Museum and the University Museum in Philadelphia to digitize all the available information on the excavations and the finds.* The two museums hope to involve the Iraqi Museum, too, as the work progresses; this would allow all the information about the site to be made available in the same place for the very first time.

In the wake of the Gulf Wars, it seems possible that in the future, when Iraq stabilizes, Ur will have another lease of life – not just digitally, but this time as a symbol of national pride and of the enduring achievements of the great variety of people who lived and worked there over the last 7,000 years. In order to achieve this, Iraqi archaeologists are working at Ur itself, undertaking a limited amount of restoration and refurbishment while preparing an application to UNESCO to have Ur inscribed as a World Heritage Site in recognition of its unique status.

---

*   I am very grateful to Dr Jane Moon and Dr Haider alMamori for this information.

Timelines

Ur in the Ancient World

Approximate dates BC	Name of period	Major remains at Ur
6000	Ubaid	Flood level Pottery in pits X & Y etc.
5000	Uruk	Graves. Kiln strata
4000	Jemdat Nasr	Graves. Houses Pit F
3000	Early Dynastic 1	Seal impressions SIS 6/7
2800	Early Dynastic II?	Houses Pit F level E
2600	Early Dynastic IIIa/b	Royal graves and much of Royal cemetery. Ziggurat?
2350	Agade	Some late graves in Royal cemetery. Disk of Enheduanna, stone vase frags
2100	Ur III	The ziggurat and sacred temenos including empty Royal graves. Town houses
2000	Isin-Larsa period, sometimes called Early Old Baylonian period	Destruction by the Elamites
1900	Old Babylonian period Hammurabi stela.	Majority of the town houses etc. City wall. Bastion of Warad-Sin. Remains at Diqdiqqa
1700	Kassite period	Destruction level, c. 1750
1300	Assyrian period Kings of Assyria appoint puppet kings	Much rebuilding of the temenos and the *Edublalmah*. City wall
900	Followed by Sealand/Chaldaean dynasty?	Some rebuilding and remodelling of sacred area
660	Assyrian empire Governor Sin-balassu-iqbi	Remodelling and rebuilding
550	Neo-Babylonian empire	Nabonidus carries out massive works now much eroded including/?adding extra stages to the ziggurat and covering the shrine on top with glazed blue bricks. Palace of the high priestess
539	Persian conquest	Cyrus captures Babylon. Heavy erosion, but some remains of repairs. Graves

The Rediscovery of Ur

Dates	People	Major developments
1625	Pietro della Valle	Visits site and brings inscribed bricks back to Italy
1835	Colonel Cheney	Expedition for the survey of the rivers Euphrates and Tigris
1835	J. Baillie Fraser	Visits Ur and paces out dimensions of ziggurat without identifying it
1849	W. Loftus	Visits Ur and Uruk, carries out short excavation at Uruk
1854 1855	J. E. Taylor, vice-consul at Basra	Brief seasons of excavation allow him to describe ziggurat and to find four foundation inscriptions of Nabonidus
1857	Sir H. Rawlinson, Edward Hincks, W. Fox Talbot and Julius Oppert	Competition to translate cuneiform inscription. Results so similar between Rawlinson and Hincks that it was judged cuneiform had been 'cracked'
1918	R. Campbell Thompson	Initial assessment of Ur for British Museum
1919	H. R. Hall	Sent by British Museum to carry out successful season of excavation, but lack of money closes project
1922	G. B. Gordon of the University Museum Philadelphia	Proposes joint excavation with British Museum under the direction of Leonard Woolley
1922 autumn	Leonard Woolley	First season of excavations at Ur. Twelve more seasons were to follow
1934	Leonard Woolley	Final season of excavation at Ur
1935	Leonard Woolley	Woolley awarded knighthood

Further Reading

Chapter 1

There are a number of works on the history of archaeological exploration in Mesopotamia, but one of the most readable is still Seton Lloyd, *Foundations in the Dust* (rev. edn) (London: Thames and Hudson, 1980). The biblical evidence is reviewed by H. W. F. Saggs in an article entitled 'Ur of the Chaldees' in a special number of the journal *Iraq* called *Ur in Retrospect*, XXII (1960), pp. 200–9. H. R. Hall gives a very useful summary of previous work at Ur and a vivid description of digging there and at al Ubaid in H. R. Hall, *A Season's Work at Ur* (London: Methuen, 1930). Leonard Woolley has a Wikipedia entry and there is a biography by H. V. F. Winstone, *Woolley of Ur* (London: Martin Secker and Warburg, 1990). Woolley also published a charming memoir in 1962 called *As I Seem to Remember* (London: Allen and Unwin), and a book called *Digging Up the Past* (Harmondsworth: Pelican, 1954), which he describes as an introduction to archaeology, but which is now of purely historical interest. The second edition of his book *Ur of the Chaldees*, edited by P. R. S. Moorey and published in London by the Herbert Press in 1982, is essential reading for anyone interested in Ur.

The physical background is well described in J. Pournelle, 'From KLM to CORONA: a bird's eye view of cultural ecology and early Mesopotamian urbanization', in E. Stone (ed.), *Settlement and Society: Essays Dedicated to Robert McCormick Adams* (Chicago: Cotsen Institute of Archaeology, University of California and the Oriental Institute, 2007, pp. 29–63); also in Harriet Crawford (ed.), *Physical Geography in the Sumerian World* (London: Routledge, 2012, pp. 13–32); and in D. T. Potts, *Mesopotamian Civilization: The Material Foundations* (London: Athlone Press, 1997).

Chapter 2

Two excellent introductions to the archaeology of Mesopotamia are Hans J. Nissen, *The Early History of the Ancient Near East* (Chicago: University of Chicago Press, 1988) and J. N. Postgate, *Early Mesopotamia* (London: Routledge, 1992). Michael Roaf, *Cultural Atlas of Mesopotamia* (New York: Facts on File Inc., 1990 and reprints), has excellent maps and a huge amount of information.

The details of the finds at al Ubaid and Ur itself come from the excavation reports on work there by Henry R. Hall and C. Leonard Woolley, *Al-Ubaid: Ur Excavations*

Volume 1 (Oxford: Oxford University Press, 1927) and by L. Woolley, *Ur Excavations Volume 4: The Early Periods* (Oxford: Oxford University Press, 1955). The present state of research is summarized in the introduction to the most recent scholarly report on a conference held in Durham in 2006 and published as Robert A. Carter and Graham Philip (eds), 'Beyond the Ubaid: Transformation and integration in the late prehistoric societies of the Middle East', *Studies in Ancient Oriental Civilization,* no. 63 (Chicago, IL: Oriental Institute of Chicago, 2010).

Chapter 3

Detailed information on Woolley's discoveries can be found in Volume IV of the Ur excavation reports and in more digestible form in the chapter called 'From the Uruk to the Early Dynastic III period' in his *Ur of the Chaldees*, revised and updated by P. R. S. Moorey in 1982 and published by the Herbert Press. On the Uruk period, G. Algaze, *The Uruk World System* (Chicago, IL: Chicago University Press, 1993) is an admirable condensation of much archaeological detail, while the same author's *Ancient Mesopotamia at the Dawn of Civilization* (Chicago, IL: Chicago University Press, 2008) is more theoretical and looks at the reasons for the Uruk blossoming. Gil Stein, *Rethinking World Systems* (Tucson, AZ: Arizona University Press, 1999) makes some important modifications to Algaze's ideas. In 2001, M. Rothman edited a valuable book called *Uruk Mesopotamia and its Neighbours* (Santa Fe and Oxford: School of American Research Advanced Seminar Series), which is the result of a conference on the same theme and is rather academic.

An excellent account of the uses of the earliest tablets can be found in H. Nissen, P. Damerow and Robert Englund, *Archaic Bookkeeping* (Chicago, IL: Chicago University Press, 1993).

Chapter 4

An authoritative discussion of the city sealings with copious references can be seen in R. J. Matthews, *Cities, Seals and Writing: Archaic Seal Impressions from Jemdat Nasr and Ur.* (Berlin: Gebr. Mann Verla, 1993).

A very useful introduction to urban Mesopotamia is Marc Van de Mieroop's *The Mesopotamian City* (Oxford, Clarendon Press, 1997).

Susan Pollock has some very interesting things to say in her 1999 *Ancient Mesopotamia* (Cambridge: Cambridge University Press, 1999).

Brief accounts of the history of the period can be found in books such as Amelie Kuhrt's two-volume *The Ancient Near East* (London: Routledge, 1995) and W. W. Hallo and W. K. Simpson, *The Ancient Near East: A History,* 2nd ed. (New York: Harcourt Brace, 1998).

The definitive edition of the Sumerian King List is still T. Jacobsen's edition published in 1939 by Chicago. With certain reservations, he sees the list as an historical source. P. Michalowski on the other hand regards the King List as pure propaganda, having no historical value. See his 'History as Charter', *Journal of the American Oriental Society*, vol. 103 (1983), pp. 237–48.

For the royal cemetery there is a general summary in P. R. S. Moorey's revised edition of Leonard Woolley's *Ur of the Chaldees* (London Herbert Press, 1982), referred to in earlier chapters. For the full report, which includes the specialists' reports on inscriptions, metals and bone as well as a detailed description of the architecture and the finds, see C. L. Woolley, *Ur Excavations Volume II: The Royal Cemetery* (London and Philadelphia: British Museum and Museum of the University, 1934). This covers the private graves as well.

More recently an excellent exhibition catalogue deals with the Royal graves and their contents: R. L. Zettler and Lee Horne, *Treasures from the Royal Tombs of Ur* (Seattle: Marquand, 1998).

Recent research on the human remains can be found in the *Cambridge Archaeological Journal*, vol.21.3 (2011), pp. 427–45 in an article by Massimo Vidale called 'PG 1237, Royal Cemetery of Ur: Patterns in Death'. See also the journal by Aubery Baadsgaard et al., 'Human Sacrifice and Intentional Corpse Preservation in the Royal Cemetery at Ur', *Antiquity*, vol. 85.3 (2011), pp. 27–42.

For the suggestion that those buried in the cemetery were members of the entourages of the primary interments in the royal graves, see Susan Pollock, 'Of Priestesses, Princes and Poor Relations: The Dead in the Royal Cemetery of Ur', *Cambridge Archaelogical Journal*, vol. 1.2 (1991), pp. 171–89.

For the ideas about the burials as an intrinsic tool for establishing the institution of kingship see A. C. Cohen, *Death Rituals, Ideology, and the Development of Early Mesopotamian Kingship* (Leiden: Brill, 2005).

Chapter 5

The most detailed descriptions of the objects from the graves can be found in *Ur Excavations II* and the revised edition of *Ur of the Chaldees*. The Zettler and Horne exhibition catalogue, *Treasures from the Royal Tombs of Ur*, referenced in Chapter 4's notes, has magnificent pictures and important essays on the different categories of artefacts.

An excellent reference work is P. R. S. Moorey, *Mesopotamian Materials and Industries* (Oxford: Clarendon Press, 1994).

Chapter 6

The history of the rise and fall of the Agade kings is described in Amelie Kuhrt, *The Ancient Near East*, 2 vols (London: Routledge, 1995) and in very concise form in Hallo and Simpson's *The Ancient Near East*.

For the archaeology, the two most important sources remain Woolley's two volumes on the royal cemetery and the second edition of *Ur of the Chaldees* revised by P. R. S. Moorey (for details see notes on Chapter 4).

For an introduction to the history of cylinder seals, see Dominique Collon, *First Impressions: Cylinder Seals in the Ancient Near East* (London: British Museum Press, 1987).

For the art of the period see one of the surveys by H. Frankfort, *Art and Architecture of the Ancient Orient* (Harmondsworth: Penguin Books, 1954 and later revisions) or A. Moortgat, *The Art of Ancient Mesopotamia* (London: Phaidon, 1969). More specialized is P. Amiet, *L'art d'Agadé* (Paris: Musées Nationaux, 1976).

Chapter 7

C. L. Woolley, *Ur Excavations Volume V: The Ziggurat and its Surroundings* (London: British Museum Press, 1939) and *Ur Excavations Volume VI: The Buildings of the Third Dynasty* (Philadelphia: University of Pennslyvania Press, 1974). See also the second edition of *Ur of the Chaldees* revised by P. R. S. Moorey.

There are a number of scholarly articles about the individual buildings, such as Penelope N. Weadock, 'The Giparu at Ur', *Iraq*, vol. 37, no. 2 (1975), pp. 101–28. Moorey has also written an article on the Ur III royal graves: 'Where did they Bury the Kings of the Third Dynasty of Ur?' *Iraq*, vol. 46, no. 1, pp. 1–18.

Many aspects of the Ur III state are covered in an excellent volume by McG. Gibson and R. D. Biggs (eds), *The Organization of Power: Aspects of Bureaucracy in the Ancient Near East* (2nd edn), *Studies in Ancient Oriental Civilization*, no. 46 (Chicago: Oriental Institute University of Chicago, 1991).

For the death of Ur-Nammu, see J. Black et al. (eds), *The Literature of Ancient Sumer* (Oxford: Oxford University Press, 2004, pp. 56–62); for the death of Gilgamesh/Bilgamesh, see Andrew George, *The Epic of Gilgamesh* (Harmondsworth: Penguin, 1999).

For the lamentation over the destruction of Sumer and Ur, see Piotr Michalowski (ed.), *The Lamentation Over the Destruction of Sumer and Ur* (Winona Lake, IN: Eisenbrauns, 1989).

For the Ur-Nammu stela, see J. V. Canby, *The Ur-Nammu Stela*, Pennsylvania University Museum Monographs, X (Philadelphia: Pennsylvania University Press, 2001).

For the description of the ziggurat at Babylon, see Herodotus, *Histories*, 1.

Chapter 8

Sir L. Woolley and Sir Max Mallowan, *Ur VII: The Old Babylonian Period* (London: British Museum Press, 1976). and Moorey's revised edition of Woolley's *Ur of the Chaldees.*

For the history, see Amelie Kuhrt, *The Ancient Near East* referenced in the notes for Chapter 4. A shorter and perhaps more digestible account is given in Hallo and Simpson's *The Ancient Near East.* See M. Mallowan, *Mallowan's Memoirs* (London: Collins, 1977) for the description of Woolley showing visitors round the houses. See also Marc Van de Mieroop's *The Ancient Mesopotamian City*, referenced in Chapter 4's notes.

For a summary of relations with Dilmun and further references see D. T. Potts, *The Arabian Gulf in Antiquity*, vol. 1 (Oxford: Clarendon Press, 1990) and, rather less scholarly, Harriet Crawford, *Dilmun and its Gulf Neighbours* (Cambridge: Cambridge University Press, 1998).

For an analysis of the 'permeability' etc. of the houses: Paolo Brusasco, 'Family Archives and the Social Use of Space in Old Babylonian Houses at Ur', Mesopotamia, vols 34–5 (1999), pp. 3–174.

For the taxation policies and reform of the bureaucracy by Ur-Nammu and Shulgi: see Gibson and Biggs's *The Organization of Power*, referenced in the notes for Chapter 7.

For the lamentation over the destruction of Sumer and Ur, see Piotr Michalowski's *The Lamentation Over the Destruction of Sumer and Ur*, referenced in the notes for Chapter 7.

Chapter 9

Moorey's edition of Woolley is the best introduction, while a more detailed account can be found in Sir Leonard Woolley, *Ur Excavations Volume VIII: The Kassite Period and the Period of the Assyrian Kings* (London: British Museum Press, 1965), and in his *The Ziggurat and its Surroundings.*

For the history see Amelie Kuhrt's *The Ancient Near East.* (2 vols) (London: Routledge, 1995).

A general survey of the periods covered in this chapter can be found in D. T. Potts (ed.), *A Companion to the Archaeology of the Ancient Near East,* vol. 2 (Oxford: Blackwell, 2012), especially chapters by M. Heinz on the kings of the Ur III, Old Babylonian and Kassite 'empires', and H. Baker on the Neo-Babylonian Empire.

For an introduction to Assyrian sculpture: Julian Reade, *Assyrian Sculpture* (London: British Museum Press, 1983).

A new translation of Herodotus by Tom Holland was published in 2013 by Penguin.

Chapter 10

As usual, the best sources of information on the archaeology of the Neo-Babylonian and Persian periods are to be found in C. L. Woolley and Max Mallowan, *Ur Excavations Volume IX: The Neo-Babylonian and Persian Periods* (London: British Museum Press, 1962), and Moorey's second edition of *Ur of the Chaldees.*

For an account of the actions taken by the allies after the invasion of 2003, see Peter Stone and Joanne F. Bajjaly (eds), *The Destruction of Cultural Heritage in Iraq* (Woodbridge: Boydell, 2008).

For a very readable account of his own work, see Matthew Bogdanos, *Thieves of Baghdad* (New York: Bloomsbury, 2005).

For the damage at Ur, see John Curtis, *British Museum – Ur report 2007,* www.britishmuseum.org/.../middle_east/iraq_projet/ur_report_2007.aspx (last accessed 5/10/13).

The progress of work at Tell Khaiber can be followed at www.urarchaeology.org

Index